U.S. Chart No. 1

Symbols, Abbreviations and Terms used on Paper and Electronic Navigational Charts

 13th Edition
April 15, 2019

Prepared Jointly by

Department of Commerce
National Oceanic and Atmospheric Administration

Department of Defense
National Geospatial-Intelligence Agency

Presented by
Paradise Cay Publications Inc.
PO Box 29
Arcata, CA 95518-0029

Phone: (707) 822-9063
Fax: (707) 822-9163
orders@paracay.com
www.paracay.com
Printed in U.S.A.

ECDIS Symbols and Other ECDIS Information

Symbology for displaying Electronic Navigational Charts (ENCs) on Electronic Chart Display and Information Systems (ECDIS) has been added to U.S. Chart No. 1. In addition to the ECDIS symbols shown in the traditional lettered sections of U.S. Chart No. 1, there are now several special pages devoted exclusively to providing important details about ECDIS. These pages are distinguished by the ECDIS icon, as shown in the top left corner of this page. The ECDIS pages are also listed in the table of contents in italic type.

 One major difference in the use of paper charts and ENCs is the ability of ECDIS to display the same feature differently depending on user settings and other conditions, such as a ship's draft. An important example is that ECDIS displays wrecks, rocks and other obstructions with their traditional "paper chart" symbols if they are at or deeper than the depth of the safety contour set for the ship. Dangers that are shoaler are portrayed with the unique ECDIS "isolated danger" symbol shown at left. (See the ECDIS Portrayal of Depths page for more information about the ECDIS safety contour.)

 Another advantage that ECDIS provides over paper charts is enabling users to obtain more information about a feature through a "cursor pick." Some feature attribute values that can be obtained by cursor pick are noted throughout U.S. Chart No. 1. This is especially true if a particular value, such as height, vertical clearance or the like is included in the INT symbol description. The cursor pick icon, shown at left, is used to indicate when a reference to a cursor pick is made.

There are many other attribute values that users may obtain through a cursor pick that are not specifically noted. These include, but are not limited to, the purpose, seasonality, periodicity, status, color, height, type of structure and the visual or radar conspicuousness of features; shape, color or color pattern of buoys; characteristics of lights; category of obstructions and wrecks; radar wave length, radio frequency, communication channel and call signs; the presence of AIS transmitted signals; information regarding pilotage services and many more.

U.S. Chart No. 1 is a handy guide for ECDIS users, but it is no substitute for mandated ECDIS training.

The ECDIS user and developer communities are invited to help improve the presentation of ECDIS symbology and information in U.S. Chart No. 1. Please ley us know what additional information you would like to see in the next edition.

Corrections, comments, or questions regarding U.S. Chart No. 1 may be submitted through ASSIST, the NOAA Coast Survey stakeholder engagement and feedback website at *www.nauticalcharts.noaa.gov/customerservice/assist*,

or mailed to:

National Ocean Service, NOAA (N/CS2)
Attention: U.S. Chart No. 1
1315 East West Highway
Silver Spring, MD 20912-3282

SYMBOLS, ABBREVIATIONS AND TERMS
Contents

Document Sections and *ECDIS Pages*

Introduction	5
Schematic Layout	8
Day, Dusk and Night Color Palettes	9
Conspicuous and Non-Conspicuous Features	28
ECDIS Portrayal of Depths	47
Examples of Routing Measures in ECDIS	69
Simplified and Traditional "Paper Chart" Symbols	90
Index of Abbreviations	111
Index	117
Appendix 1, IALA Maritime Buoyage System	128

Symbol Sections

GENERAL
- A   Chart Number, Title, Marginal Notes
- B   Positions, Distances, Directions, Compass

TOPOGRAPHY
- C   Natural Features
- D   Cultural Features
- E   Landmarks
- F   Ports
- G   (Not currently used)

HYDROGRAPHY
- H   Tides, Currents
- I   Depths
- J   Nature of the Seabed
- K   Rocks, Wrecks, Obstructions, Aquaculture
- L   Offshore Installations
- M   Tracks, Routes
- N   Areas, Limits
- O   (Not currently used)

NAVIGATION AIDS AND SERVICES
- P   Lights
- Q   Buoys, Beacons
- R   Fog Signals
- S   Radar, Radio, Satellite Navigation Systems
- T   Services
- U   Small Craft (Leisure) Facilities

INTRODUCTION

Two Symbology Types Comprising Four Symbology Sets

U.S. Chart No. 1 presents two types of symbology used for marine navigation – the symbols used on paper nautical charts (and their digital raster image equivalents) and the corresponding symbols used to portray Electronic Navigational Chart (ENC) data on Electronic Chart Display and Information Systems (ECDIS).

Within these two types, four separate symbology sets are shown. These are described below:

Paper Chart Symbols

INT — The international or "INT" symbols specified in the *Regulations for International (INT) Charts and Chart Specifications of the IHO* (International Hydrographic Organization). These symbols are used by many countries around the world, including the United States.

NOAA — Symbols used on charts produced by the National Oceanic and Atmospheric Administration (NOAA) when an INT symbol is not used. NOAA produces nautical charts for all U.S. waters, including the Great Lakes and U.S. Territories.

NGA — Symbols used on charts produced by the National Geospatial-Intelligence Agency (NGA) when an INT symbol is not used. NGA produces nautical charts for the U.S. military and for areas outside of U.S. waters.

ECDIS Symbols

ECDIS — Symbols used to portray ENCs on ECDIS navigation systems. Use of ECDIS is required for large commercial ships on international voyages. These symbols are specified in *IHO Specifications for Chart Content and Display Aspects of ECDIS*.

Other Non-ECDIS Digital Displays May Portray Data Differently

Navigation systems certified to meet the exacting performance standards established by the International Maritime Organization (IMO) are said to be ECDIS "type approved." The symbology used to display ENCs or other non-ENC navigational data on non-ECDIS systems, such as geographic information systems, recreational GPS and other chart display systems can differ significantly from the symbology specified for ECDIS type approved systems. U.S. Chart No. 1 only shows the symbology used on ECDIS.

U.S. Chart No. 1 and Typical Chart Layouts

A brief description of the columns on each symbol description page is provided here. A detailed schematic layout of U.S. Chart No. 1 is on page 8. Section A, on pages 10 and 11 presents schematics showing typical layouts of the major elements of NOAA and NGA charts.

Col 1 — Symbol number. The number together with the section letter which appears at the top of each page constitutes a unique identifier for each symbol, such as C1 for the "Coastline, surveyed" symbol.

Col 2 — INT symbol example.

Col 3 — Description of the feature or real world phenomenon being portrayed.

Col 4 — NOAA symbol example. This column will be blank if NOAA uses the INT symbol shown in column 2.

Col 5 — NGA symbol example. This column will be blank if NGA uses the INT symbol shown in column 2.

If columns 4 and 5 are combined, then NOAA and NGA both use the same symbol, which is different from the INT symbol.

Col 6 — Other NGA symbol examples. NGA produces facsimiles of some foreign charts. If the depiction on the chart is different than the INT or NGA symbols (shown in Cols 2 and 5, respectively) then the additional foreign symbols are shown here.

Col 7 — ECDIS symbol example in the day color palettes. (See page 9 for a description of ECDIS color palettes.)

Col 8 — The ECDIS description usually provides the generic symbol name given in the *IHO Specifications for Chart Content and Display Aspects of ECDIS*, although sometimes other clarifying terms are also provided.

The schematic layout on page 7 shows a typical symbol table page and provides more details about the table headers and the types of information presented in each of the columns.

INFORMATION ON SELECTED CHART FEATURES

Soundings

The sounding datum reference is stated in the chart title. Soundings on NOAA and NGA charts may be shown in fathoms, feet, fathoms and feet, fathoms and fractions, or meters and decimeters. In all cases the unit of depth used is shown in the chart title and outside the border of the chart in bold type (see item b in Section A). For ECDIS, the sounding datum is part of the ENC metadata, which can be retrieved through a cursor inquiry.

Heights

Heights of lights, landmarks, structures, etc. refer to the shoreline plane of reference. The unit of height is shown in the chart title. When the elevations of islets or bare rocks are offset into the adjacent water, they are shown in parentheses. For ECDIS, the unit of height is meters.

Drying Heights

For rocks and banks that cover and uncover, elevations are underlined and are referenced to the sounding datum as stated in the chart title (or in the ENC metadata). When the heights of rocks that cover and uncover are offset into the adjacent water, they are shown in parentheses.

Shoreline

Shoreline shown on charts represents the line of contact between the land and a selected water elevation. In areas affected by tidal fluctuation, this line of contact is usually the mean high water line. In confined coastal waters of diminished tidal influence, a mean water level may be used. The shoreline of interior waters (rivers, lakes) is usually a line representing a specified elevation above a selected datum. Shoreline is symbolized by a heavy line (symbol C 1). Apparent shoreline is used on charts to show the outer edge of marine vegetation where the limit would be expected to appear as the shoreline to the mariner or where it prevents the shoreline from being clearly defined. Apparent shoreline is symbolized by a light line (symbols C 32, C 33, C p, C q and C r).

Landmarks

A structure or a conspicuous feature on a structure may be shown by a landmark symbol with a descriptive label (see Section E). Prominent buildings that could assist the mariner may be shown by actual shape as viewed from above (see Sections D and E).

On NGA charts, landmark legends shown in capital letters indicate that a landmark is conspicuous; the landmark may also be labeled "CONSPICUOUS" or "CONSPIC." On NOAA charts, all landmarks are considered to be conspicuous, and landmark legends shown in all capital letters indicate a landmark has been positioned accurately; legends using both upper and lower case letters indicate an approximate position.

ECDIS portrays conspicuous features with black symbols and non-conspicuous features with brown symbols. Only the conspicuous version is shown in the lettered sections of U.S. Chart No. 1. See the ECDIS "Conspicuous and Non-Conspicuous Features" page in front of Section E for more information.

IALA Buoyage System

The International Association of Marine Aids to Navigation and Lighthouse Authorities (IALA) Maritime Buoyage System is followed by most of the world's maritime nations; however, systems used in some foreign waters may be different. IALA buoyage is divided into two regions: Region A and Region B. All navigable waters of the United States follow IALA Region B rules, except U.S. possessions west of the International Date Line and south of 10° north latitude, which follow IALA Region A rules.

The major difference between the two buoyage regions is the color of the lateral marks. Region A uses red to port and Region B uses red to starboard (red-right-returning). The shapes of the lateral marks are the same in both regions, can to port and cone (nun) to starboard, when entering from seaward. Cardinal and other marks, such as those for isolated dangers, safe water and special marks are also the same in both regions. Section Q and Appendix 1 illustrate the IALA buoyage system for both Regions A and B.

U.S. Lateral Marks

Most of U.S. waters are in IALA Region B. In the U.S. system, on entering a channel from seaward, buoys and beacon dayboards on the starboard side are red with even numbers and have red lights, if lit. Buoys and beacon dayboards on the port side are green with odd numbers and have green lights, if lit. Preferred channel buoys have red and green horizontal bands with the top band color indicating the preferred side of passage.

Light Range (Visibility)

A light's range or visibility is given in nautical miles, except on the Great Lakes and adjacent waterways, where light ranges are given in statute miles. For lights having more than one color, NOAA charts give only the shortest range of all the colors. On NGA charts, multiple ranges may be shown using the following convention. For lights with two colors, the first number indicates the range of the first color and the second number indicates the range of the second color. For example, Fl WG 12/8M means the range of the white light is 12 nautical miles and the range of green light is 8 nautical miles. For lights with three colors, only the longest and shortest ranges are given and the middle range is indicated by a dash. For example, Fl WRG 12-8M means that the range of the white light is 12 nautical miles, the range of green light is 8 nautical miles and the range of the red light is between 8 to 12 nautical miles. The dash can appear in any of the three positions.

Aids to Navigation Positioning

The fixed and floating aids to navigation depicted on charts have varying degrees of reliability. Floating aids are moored to sinkers by varying lengths of chain and may shift due to sea conditions and other causes. Buoys may also be carried away, capsized or sunk. Lighted buoys may be extinguished and sound signals may not function, because of ice or other causes. Therefore, prudent mariners will not rely solely on any single aid to navigation, particularly on floating aids, but will also use bearings from fixed objects and aids to navigation on shore.

Colors

Color conveys the nature and importance of features found on nautical charts. Chart elements significant to marine navigation, such as lights, compass roses and regulated areas, are emphasized with magenta. Lateral marks on NOAA charts are shown with a red or green fill. Shades of blue depict potential hazards to navigation, typically shallow water and submerged obstructions. Areas of deeper water believed to be clear of obstructions are shown as white. Land, and other features that are always dry, are depicted with buff on NOAA charts and gray on NGA charts. Foreshore and other intertidal features are portrayed with a green tint. Other colors may be used to provide additional information, such as protected areas, which are outlined in blue or green.

Traffic Separation Schemes

Traffic separation schemes show recommended lanes to increase safety of navigation, particularly in areas of high density shipping. These schemes are described in the International Maritime Organization (IMO) publication, *Ships Routeing*. Traffic separation schemes are generally shown on nautical charts at scales of 1:600,000 and larger. When possible, traffic separation schemes are plotted to scale and shown as depicted in Section M.

Conversion Scales

Depth conversion scales are provided on all charts to enable the user to work in meters, fathoms or feet.

Correction Date

The date of each new chart edition is shown below the lower left border of the chart. The date of the latest NGA issued U.S. Notice to Mariners applied to the chart is shown after the edition date. NOAA charts also show the date of the latest U.S. Coast Guard Local Notice to Mariners applied to the chart.

ADDITIONAL RESOURCES

Information on the use of nautical charts, aids to navigation, sounding datums and the practice of navigation in general is in *The American Practical Navigator* (Bowditch), available through the "Publications" link on the NGA Maritime Safety Information portal at https://msi.nga.mil/NGAPortal/MSI.portal.

Tide and current data over U.S. waters is available from the NOAA Center for Operational Oceanographic Products and Services at https://tidesandcurrents.noaa.gov.

Detailed information about specific lights, buoys, and beacons and general information about the U.S. Aids to Navigation System and the Uniform State Waterway Marking Systems is in the U.S. Coast Guard *Light List,* at https//www.navcen.uscg.gov/?pageName=lightLists.

Information about aids to navigation in foreign waters is in the NGA *List of Lights,* available through the "Publications" link on the NGA Maritime Safety Information portal at https://msi.nga.mil/NGAPortal/MSI.portal.

Other important information that cannot be shown conveniently on nautical charts can be found in the NOAA *U.S. Coast Pilot*®, at https://nauticalcharts.noaa.gov/publications/coast-pilot/index.html and NGA *Sailing Directions,* available through the "Publications" link on the NGA Maritime Safety Information portal at https://msi.nga.mil/NGAPortal/MSI.portal.

U.S. Nautical Chart Catalogs and Indexes

NGA catalogs are available through the "Product Catalog" link on the NGA Maritime Safety Information portal at https://msi.nga.mil/NGAPortal/MSI.portal.

NOAA catalogs are available at the NOAA Chart Locator at

www.charts.noaa.gov/InteractiveCatalog/nrnc.shtml and the NOAA Nautical Chart Catalog and Chart Viewer at www.charts.noaa.gov/ChartCatalog/MapSelect.html.

A list of the dates of the latest editions of NOAA charts is at https://nauticalcharts.noaa.gov/charts/list-of-latest-editions.html.

CORRECTIONS AND COMMENTS

Corrections to U.S. Chart No. 1 will appear in the weekly U.S. Notice to Mariners, available through the "Notice to Mariners" link on the NGA Maritime Safety Information portal at https://msi.nga.mil/NGAPortal/MSI.portal.

Corrections, comments, or questions regarding U.S. Chart No. 1 may be submitted through ASSIST, the NOAA Coast Survey stakeholder engagement and feedback website at www.nauticalcharts.noaa.gov/customer-service/assist.

or to:

National Ocean Service, NOAA (N/CS2)
Attention: U.S. Chart No. 1
1315 East West Highway
Silver Spring, MD 20910-3282

Schematic Layout of U.S. Chart No. 1:

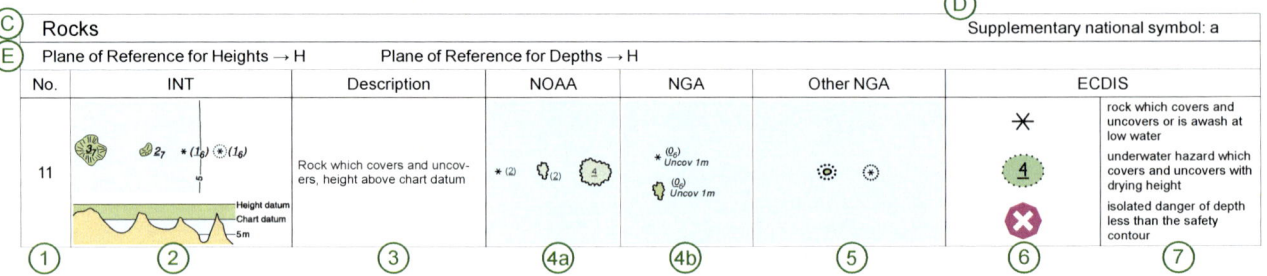

Ⓐ	Section designation
Ⓑ	Section
Ⓒ	Sub-section
Ⓓ	Reference to "Supplementary national symbols" at the end of each section
Ⓔ	Cross-reference to terms in other sections
①	Column 1: Numbering system following the "Chart Specification of the IHO". A letter in this column indicates a supplementary national symbol or abbreviation for which there is no international equivalent.
②	Column 2: Representation that follows the "Chart Specifications of the IHO" (INT 1 symbol)
③	Column 3: Description of symbol, term, or abbreviation
④a *	Column 4a: Representation used on charts produced by the National Oceanic and Atmospheric Administration (NOAA)
④b *	Column 4b: Representation used on charts produced by the National Geospatial-Intelligence Agency (NGA)
⑤	Column 5: Representation of symbols that may appear on NGA reproductions of foreign charts
⑥ **	Column 6: Representation used to portray ENC data on ECDIS
⑦ **	Column 7: Description of ECDIS symbols

* When columns 4a and 4b are combined then NOAA and NGA both use the same symbol. When either column 4a or 4b is blank then the respective agency uses the INT 1 symbol shown in column 2.

** When columns 6 and 7 have several rows for the same symbol number, then ECDIS portrays this feature differently depending on the ship's draft and other conditions as defined in ECDIS by the mariner (as is the case for K 11). When columns 6 and 7 combine rows to span across several symbol numbers then ECDIS portrays all of the grouped symbol numbers the same way (see C 5–C 7).

† Signifies that this representation is obsolete, but it may appear on older charts.

  Signifies that a feature attribute value, such as a height, distance or name, may be obtained through an ECDIS cursor pick report. There are many attribute values that may be obtained in this manner, but the cursor pick icon is only used to note values that are specifically referred to in the description of symbols column and that ECDIS does not display next to the symbol. Height of trees in C 14 is an example.

Day, Dusk and Night Color Palettes

ECDIS allows the mariner to change the color palette that is used to display an ENC. Three different color tables have been designed to provide the maximum clarity and contrast between features on the display under three different lighting conditions on the bridge, namely Day, Dusk and Night.

Each symbol is rendered in a different color appropriate for the lighting condition that the color table is meant for. This design provides maximum contrast for the display on a sunny day, as well as preserving night vision on a dimly lit bridge in the evening. This allows the mariner to look back and forth between the chart on the ECDIS display and out to sea through the bridge window without the mariner's eyes needing to readjust to a difference in light intensity.

- The Day Color Table, meant to be used in bright sunlight, uses a white background for deep water and looks the most like a traditional paper chart.
- The Dusk Color Table uses a black background for deep water and colors are subdued, but slightly brighter than those used in the Night Color Table.
- The Night Color Table, meant to be used in the darkest conditions, uses a black background for deep water and muted color shades for other features.

The images on the right show each of the three color palettes.

The symbols shown in the remainder of this document use the day color palette.

DAY

DUSK

NIGHT

A Chart Number, Title, Marginal Notes

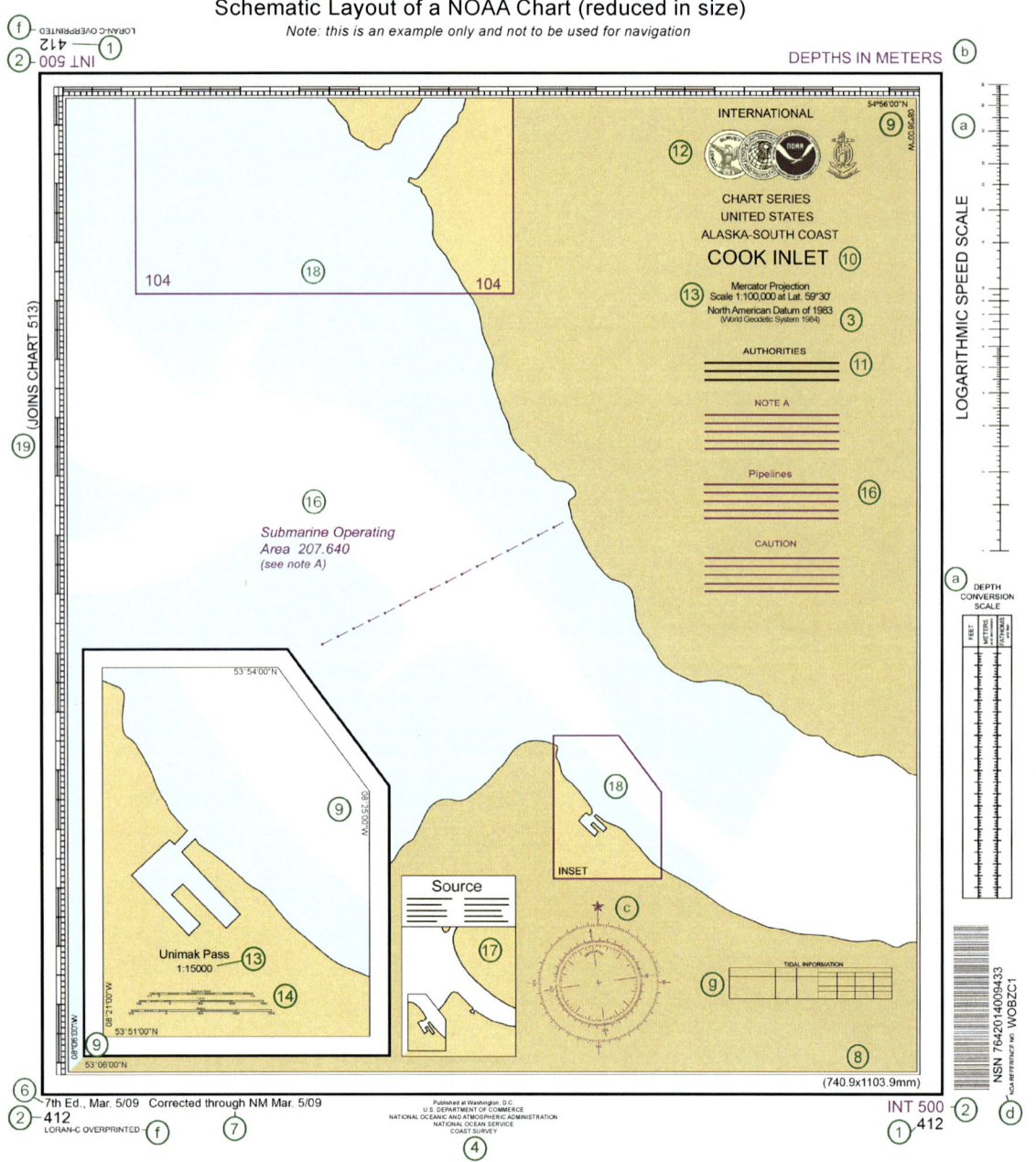

Magnetic Features → B	
Tidal Data → H	
①	Chart number in national chart series
②	Chart number in international (INT) series (if any)
③	Reference ellipsoid of the chart
④	Publication note (imprint)
⑤	Copyright note
⑥	Date of current edition
⑦	Notice to Mariners corrections
⑧	Dimensions of inner borders
⑨	Corner coordinates
⑩	Chart title
⑪	Explanatory notes on chart construction, etc. To be read before using chart.
⑫	Seal(s)
⑬	Scale of chart. Some charts have scale at a stated latitude.
⑭	Linear scale on large scale charts

Chart Number, Title, Marginal Notes A

Schematic Layout of an NGA Chart (reduced in size)
Note: this is an example only and not to be used for navigation

15	Linear border scale on large scale charts. On smaller scales use latitude borders for sea miles.
16	Cautionary notes (if any). Information on particular features, to be read before using chart.
17	Source Diagram (if any). Navigators should be cautious where surveys are inadequate.
18	Reference to a larger scale chart
19	Reference to an adjoining chart of similar scale
a	Conversion scales
b	Reference to the units used for depth measurement
c	Compass rose
d	Bar code and stock number
e	Glossary: Translation of words on chart that are not in English
g	Tidal and Tidal Stream information within the chart coverage

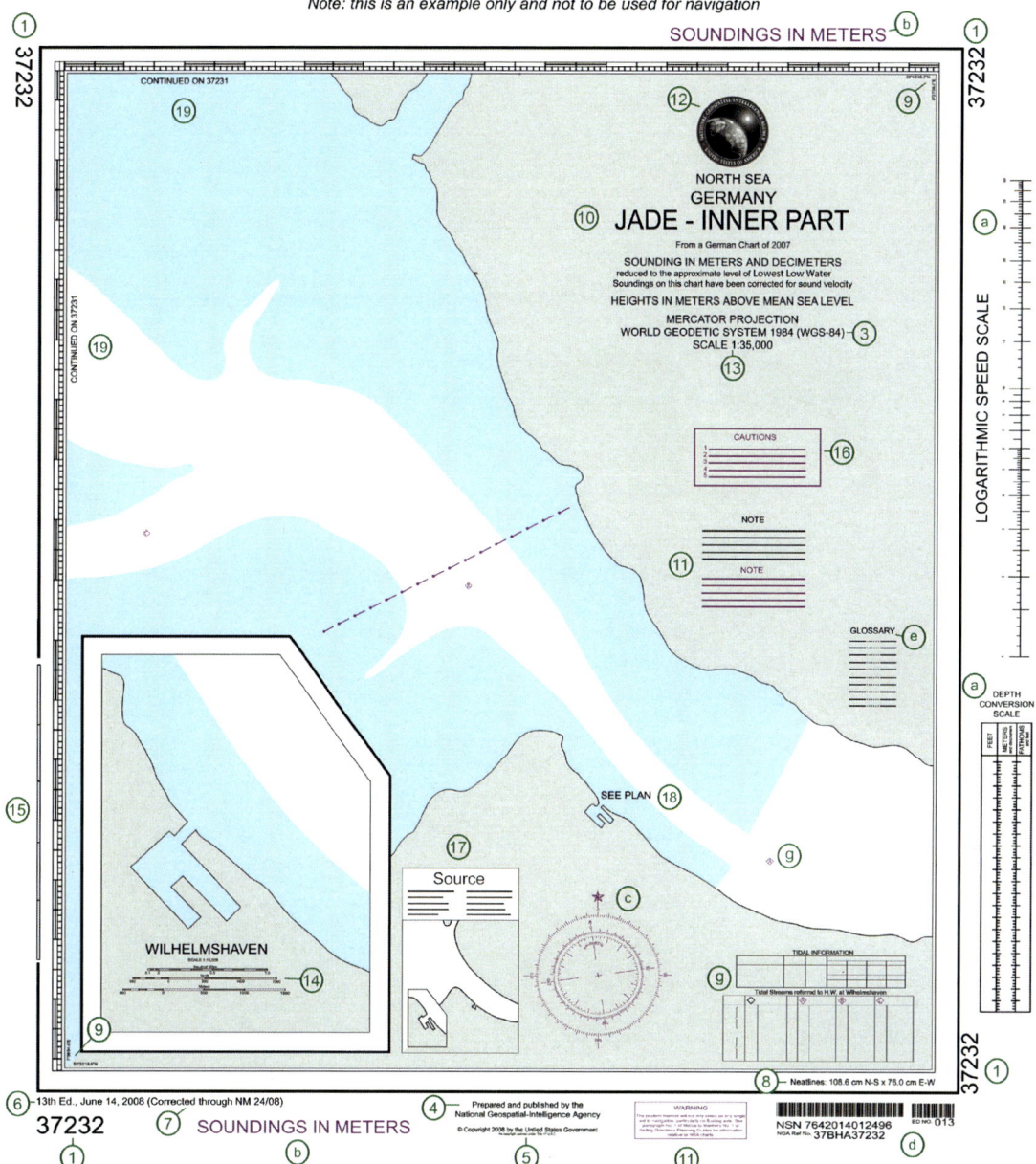

11

B Positions, Distances, Directions, Compass

No.	INT	Description	NOAA	NGA	Other NGA	ECDIS	
Geographical Positions							
1	Lat	Latitude					
2	Long	Longitude					
4		Degree(s)	deg				
5		Minute(s) of arc					
6		Second(s) of arc					
7	*PA*	Position approximate (not accurately determined or does not remain fixed)	PA	(PA)		PA	Position approximate
						?	Point feature or area of low accuracy
						21	Sounding of low accuracy
8	*PD*	Position doubtful (reported in various positions)	PD	(PD)		?	Point feature or area of low accuracy
						21	Sounding of low accuracy
9	N	North					
10	E	East					
11	S	South					
12	W	West					
13	NE	Northeast					
14	SE	Southeast					
15	NW	Northwest					
16	SW	Southwest					

Positions, Distances, Directions, Compass B

No.	INT	Description	NOAA	NGA	Other NGA	ECDIS	
Control Points							
20	△	Triangulation Point					
21	† ⊕	Observation spot	⊕ Obs Spot			○	Position of an elevation or control point
22	⊙ ⊙	Fixed point	⊙				
25.1	○ km 32	Distance along waterway, no visible marker	St M 32			km 7	Canal and distance point with no mark
25.2	○ km 46	Distance along waterway with visible marker	▢ Y Bn (46)			○ km 7	Canal and distance point
	Note: ECDIS uses a magenta "km" symbol to represent distance marks. However, the distances shown along waterways on NOAA-produced ENCs are displayed in statute miles.						
Symbolized Positions (Examples)							
30	⋈ # Wk	Symbols in plan—position is center of primary symbol				ECDIS follows the paper chart convention for the position of symbols, except for simplified symbols for buoys and beacons (see Q 1).	
31	⚓ ⚑ ⚓	Symbols in plan—position is at bottom of symbol					
32	⊙ Mast ⊙ MAST ★	Point symbols	⊙ MAST			⊙	Position of a point feature
33	† ○ Mast PA	Point symbols—approximate positions	○ Mast			ECDIS indicates approximate position only for wrecks, obstructions, islets and shoreline features.	
Units						Supplementary national symbols a–m	
40	km	Kilometer(s)					
41	m	Meter(s)					
42	dm	Decimeter(s)					
43	cm	Centimeter(s)					
44	mm	Millimeter(s)					
45	M	International nautical mile(s) (1852m), sea mile(s)	Mi	NMi	NM		
47	ft	Foot / Feet					
48	fm, fms	Fathom(s)					

B Positions, Distances, Directions, Compass

No.	INT		Description	NOAA	NGA	Other NGA	ECDIS	
49	h		Hour(s)	hr				
50	m	min	Minute(s) of time					
51	s	sec	Second(s) of time					
52	kn		Knot(s)					
53	t		Ton(s), Tonnage (weight)					
54	cd		Candela(s)					
Magnetic Compass							Supplementary national symbols *n*	
68.1	Magnetic Variation 4°30′W 2011 (8′E)		Note of magnetic variation, in position					Cursor pick site for magnetic variation at a point
								Cursor pick site for magnetic variation over an area
68.2	Magnetic Variation at 55°N 8°W 4°30′W 2011 (8′E)		Note of magnetic variation, out of position					

Positions, Distances, Directions, Compass   B

No.	NOAA / NGA		ECDIS	

70	Compass rose, normal pattern (smaller patterns of compass rose may be used)
	
	Magnetic variation (example):
	  VAR 4°15'W (2018) means magnetic variation was 4°15'W in 2018
	  ANNUAL DECREASE 8' means annual change is 8'E or decreasing 8' annually
	  For 2019 the magnetic variation is 4°7'W
				Cursor pick site for magnetic variation at a point

71	Isogonic lines, Isogonals MAGNETIC VARIATION LINES ARE FOR 2018 The magnetic variation is shown in degrees, followed by the letter W or E, as appropriate, at certain positions on the lines. The annual change is expressed in minutes with the letter W or E and is given in brackets, immediately following the variation. 3°W(5'E) 1°W(3'E) 0°(0') 1°E(3'W)		Varn - 3	Cursor pick site for magnetic variation along a line

B   Positions, Distances, Directions, Compass

No.	INT	Description	NOAA	NGA	Other NGA	ECDIS	
82.1	±15°	Local magnetic anomaly Within the enclosed area the magnetic variation may deviate from the normal by the value shown					Cursor pick site for magnetic anomaly along a line or over an area
82.2	Local Magnetic Anomaly (see Note)	Local magnetic anomaly Where the area affected cannot be easily defined, a legend only is shown at the position	LOCAL MAGNETIC DISTURBANCE (see note)	LOCAL MAGNETIC ANOMALY (see note)	LOCAL MAGNETIC DISTURBANCE (see note)		Cursor pick site for magnetic anomaly at a point
Supplementary National Symbols							
a		Square meter(s)	m²				
b		Cubic meter(s)	m³				
c		Inch(es)	in				
d		Yard(s)	yd				
e		Statute mile(s)	St M	St Mi			
f		Microsecond(s)	μsec	μs			
g		Hertz	Hz				
h		Kilohertz	kHz				
i		Megahertz	MHz				
j		Cycles/second	cps	c/s			
k		Kilocycle(s)	kc				
l		Megacycle(s)	Mc				
m		Ton(s) (U.S. short ton) (2,000lbs)	T				
o		Benchmark	BM				
p		Variation	var	VAR		Varn	Magnetic variation

Positions, Distances, Directions, Compass   B

No.	INT	Description	NOAA	NGA	Other NGA	ECDIS
q		Magnetic	mag			
r		Bearing	brg			
s		True	T			

C Natural Features

No.	INT	Description	NOAA	NGA	Other NGA	ECDIS
Coastline						Supplementary national symbols: a–e
Foreshore → I, J						
1		Coastline, surveyed				Coastline
2		Coastline, unsurveyed				Coastline or shoreline construction of low accuracy in position
3		Cliffs, Steep coast	high low † †			Presence of cliffs coincident with coastline is obtained by cursor pick / Sloping ground crest line distant from coastline, radar or visually conspicuous / Cliff as an area
4		Hillocks	†			Conspicuous hill or mountain top
5		Flat coast				
6		Sandy shore	†			Nature of coastline is obtained by cursor pick
7	Stones	Stony shore, Shingly shore	†			
8	Dunes	Sandhills, Dunes	†			Conspicuous hill or mountain top

Natural Features C

No.	INT	Description	NOAA	NGA	Other NGA	ECDIS	
Relief						Supplementary national symbols: e–g	
Plane of reference for heights → H							
10		Contour lines with values and spot height					Elevation contour with spot height, contour value is obtained by cursor pick
11		Spot heights				119 m	Position of an elevation or control point
12		Approximate contour lines with values and approximate height					
13		Form lines with spot height	†				Elevation contour with spot height, contour value is obtained by cursor pick
14		Approximate height of top of trees (above height datum)	135 TT				Approximate height of trees is obtained by cursor pick
Water Features, Lava							
20		River, Stream					River
21		Intermittent river, intermittent lake					

19

C Natural Features

No.	INT	Description	NOAA	NGA	Other NGA	ECDIS	
22		Rapids, Waterfalls					Rapids / Waterfall / Waterfall, visually conspicuous
23		Lakes					Lake
24		Salt pans					
25		Glacier	Glacier				Continuous pattern for an ice area (glacier, etc.)
26		Lava flow	Lava				

Vegetation

Supplementary national symbols: i–t

No.	INT	Description	NOAA	NGA	Other NGA	ECDIS	
30	Wooded	Woods in general	Wooded †				Line of trees / Wooded area

Natural Features   C

No.	INT	Description	NOAA	NGA	Other NGA	ECDIS	
31	Prominent trees (isolated or in groups)						
31.1		Unspecified tree					Tree
31.2		Evergreen (except conifer)					
31.3		Conifer, Casuarina					Vegetation, line of trees
31.4		Palm					
31.5		Nipa Palm					
31.6		Casuarina					Wooded area
31.7		Filao					
31.8		Eucalypt					
32		Mangrove, Nipa palm	Mangrove (used in small areas)				Mangrove with coastline or shoreline construction of low accuracy in position
33		Marsh, Swamp, Reed beds	Marsh / Swamp (used in small areas)				Marsh with coastline or shoreline construction of low accuracy in position
Supplementary National Symbols							
a		Chart sounding datum line (surveyed)	Uncovers				
b		Approximate sounding datum line (inadequately surveyed)					
c		Foreshore; Strand (in general); Stones; Shingle; Gravel; Mud; Sand	Mud				
d		Breakers along a shore	Breakers (if extensive)				

C Natural Features

No.	INT	Description	NOAA	NGA	Other NGA	ECDIS
e		Rubble	†			
f		Hachures	†			
g		Shading	†			
i		Deciduous woodland	† Wooded			
j		Coniferous woodland	† Wooded			
k		Tree plantation	†			
l		Cultivated fields	† Cultivated			
m		Grassfields	† Grass			
n		Paddy (rice) fields	† Rice			
o		Bushes	† Bushes			
p		Apparent shoreline	Marsh			
q		Vegetation or topographic (Feature Area Limit-in general)				
r		Cypress	Cypress			
s		Grass	Grass			
t		Eelgrass	Eelgrass			

Cultural Features D

No.	INT	Description	NOAA	NGA	Other NGA	ECDIS	
Settlements, Buildings							
Height of objects → E Landmarks → E							
1		Urban area					Built-up area
2		Settlement with scattered buildings					
3	○ Name ▢ Name	Settlement (on medium and small scale charts)				Name	Built-up area as a point
4	✠ Name ■ Name HOTEL	Village	Vil				
5		Buildings					Conspicuous single building
6	Hotel Hotel	Important building in built-up area					Conspicuous single building in built-up area
7	NAME	Street name, Road name					Street name is obtained by cursor pick
8	Ru Ru	Ruin, Ruined landmark	Ruins ○ Ru				Status of ruins is obtained by cursor pick
Roads, Railways, Airfields						Supplementary National Symbols: a–c	
10		Motorway, highway					Road, track or path as a line
11		Road (hard surfaced)					
12		Track, Path (loose or unsurfaced)					Road as an area

23

D   Cultural Features

No.	INT	Description	NOAA	NGA	Other NGA	ECDIS	
13		Railway, with station					Railway, with station
14		Cutting					Cutting
15		Embankment					Embankment
							Embankment, visually or radar conspicuous
16		Tunnel					Tunnel
							Tunnel with depth below the seabed encoded
17		Airport, Airfield	Airport				Airport as a point
							Runway as a line
							Airport area, with runway area and visually conspicuous runway area
18		Heliport, Helipad					
Other Cultural Features						Supplementary National Symbols: d–i	
20.1		Fixed bridge					
20.2		Footbridge, fixed bridge on smaller scale charts					

Cultural Features D

No.	INT	Description	NOAA	NGA	Other NGA	ECDIS	
21	⊢23⊣	Horizontal clearance	FIXED BRIDGE HOR CL 25 FT VERT CL 20 FT	HOR CL 8 M ⊢8⊣		Horizontal clearance is obtained by cursor pick	
22	20 (8,9)	Vertical clearance (see introduction)		VERT CL 6 M ⊺6⊥		clr 20.0 / clr 20.0	Bridge
23.1	20	Opening bridge (in general) with vertical clearance					
23.2	20	Swing bridge with vertical clearance				clr cl 8.2 clr op 20.0 / clr cl 8.2 clr op 20.0	Opening bridge
23.3	Lifting Bridge 4:2 (open 12)	Lifting bridge with vertical clearance (closed and open)					
23.4	Bascule Bridge 12	Bascule bridge with vertical clearance					
23.5	Pontoon Bridge	Pontoon bridge				clr 20.0 / clr 20.0	Bridge
23.6	Draw Bridge 5:5	Draw bridge with vertical clearance				clr cl 8.2 clr op 20.0 / clr cl 8.2 clr op 20.0	Opening bridge
24	Transporter Bridge 20	Transporter bridge with vertical clearance below fixed structure				clr 20.0 / clr 20.0	Bridge

D Cultural Features

No.	INT	Description	NOAA	NGA	Other NGA	ECDIS	
25		Overhead transporter, Aerial cableway with vertical clearance				clr 20.0	Aerial cableway
						clr 20.0	Aerial cableway, radar conspicuous
26.1		Overhead power cable with pylons and physical vertical clearance	OVERHEAD POWER CABLE AUTHORIZED CL 140 FT			sf clr 20.0	Transmission line
26.2		Overhead power cable with pylons and safe vertical clearance				sf clr 20.0	Transmission line, radar conspicuous
	Note D26.2: The safe vertical clearance defined by the responsible authority, to avoid risk of electrical discharge, has been obtained by applying a reduction to the physical vertical clearance of the cable. The reduction is variable and depends upon the transmission voltage. See H20.						
27		Overhead cable, Telephone line, with vertical clearance	Tel			clr 20.0	Overhead cable
						clr 20.0	Overhead cable, radar conspicuous
28		Overhead pipe with vertical clearance	OVHD PIPE VERT CL 6FT			clr 20.0	Overhead pipeline
						clr 20.0	Overhead pipeline, radar conspicuous
29		Pipeline on land					Oil, gas pipeline, submerged or on land
Supplementary National Symbols							
a		Highway markers					
c		Abandoned railroad					

Cultural Features D

No.	INT	Description	NOAA	NGA	Other NGA	ECDIS
d		Bridge under construction				
f		Viaduct				
g		Fence				
h		Power transmission line				
i		Approximate vertical clearance		abt 2̄1̄		

Conspicuous and Non-conspicuous Features

There are 25 features for which ECDIS displays either a black symbol, if the feature is visually conspicuous, or a brown symbol if is not. Only conspicuous landmarks are depicted on NOAA paper charts and ENCs. Therefore, only the conspicuous symbol versions are shown in the symbol tables of U.S. Chart No. 1. Both versions of the symbols for these features are shown on this page.

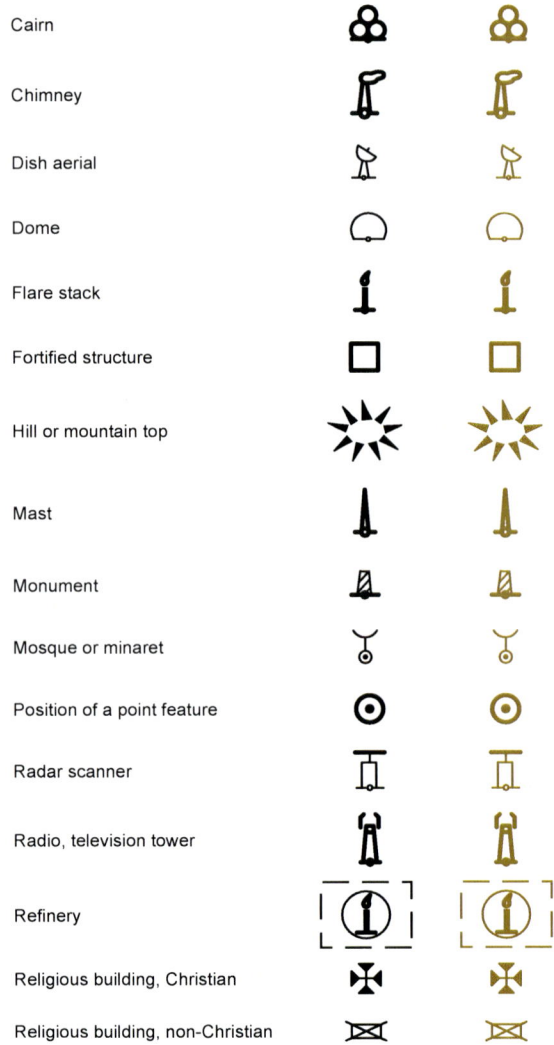

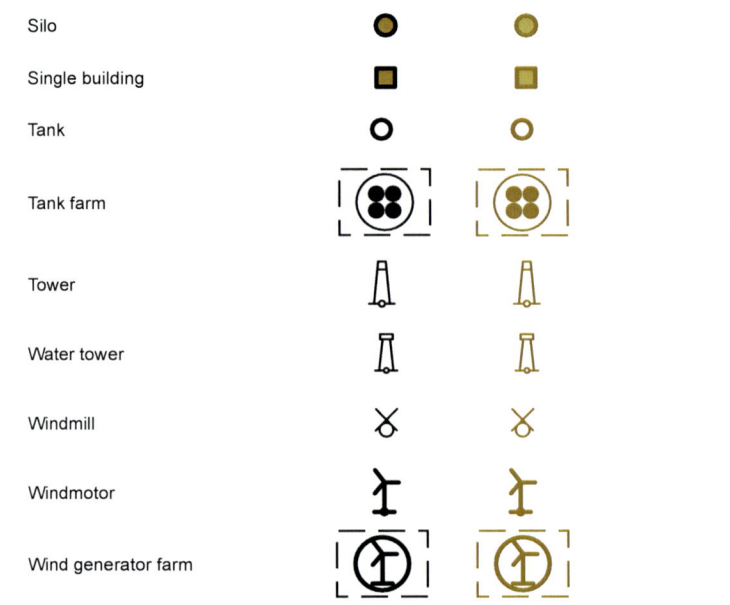

The seven symbols shown below represent features that only have a brown symbol. There is no corresponding black, conspicuous symbol. The brown symbol is displayed regardless of the conspicuousness of the feature.

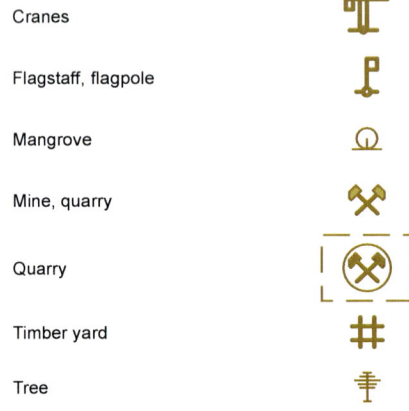

Landmarks   E

No.	INT	Description	NOAA	NGA	Other NGA	ECDIS	
Plane of Reference for Height → H		Lighthouses → P	Beacons → Q				
General							
1	◆ Factory ⌑ Hotel	Examples of landmarks	⊙ TANK ○ Tr ⊙ MONUMENT			⊙	Non-conspicuous point feature
						■	Non-conspicuous building
						⌑	Non-conspicuous water tower
2	◆ FACTORY ⊙ HOTEL ⌑ WATER TR	Examples of conspicuous landmarks (On NOAA charts, a large circle with dot and capitals indicates that position is accurate; a small circle with lowercase indicates that position is approximate.)	⊙ EMPIRE STATE BUILDING ⊙ SPIRE ⊙ RADAR MAST ⊙ CHIMNEY			⊙	Conspicuous point feature
						■	Conspicuous building
						⌑	Conspicuous water tower
3.1	🏘 🏢	Pictorial sketches (in true position)				⌑—i ✸	The information symbol is displayed if a supplemental image is available, which may be accessed by cursor pick
3.2	🏠 🏭	Pictorial sketches (out of position)					
4	⌑(30)	Height of top of a structure above height datum				✸	Height is obtained by cursor pick
5	⌑(30)	Height of structure above ground level					
Landmarks							
10.1	⌖ ✠ Ch	Church			⚓ ✝	✠	Church as a point
						⌖	Church as an area
10.2	⌖ Tr ✠ Tr	Church tower					
10.3	⌖ Sp ✠ Sp	Church spire	⊙ SPIRE ○ Spire		✝ ♁ ✝	✠	Church tower, spire, or dome
10.4	⌖ Cup ✠ Cup	Church cupola (dome)	⊙ CUPOLA ○ Cup		♀		
13	⊠	Temple, Pagoda, Shrine, Marabout, Joss house			⊕	⊠	Religious building, non-Christian

29

E Landmarks

No.	INT	Description	NOAA	NGA	Other NGA	ECDIS	
17	☿	Mosque, Minaret			☿	☿	Mosque or minaret
19	(cemetery symbol)	Cemetery	Cem	†††	⊔⊔	▢ ✦	Landmark area, type is obtained by cursor pick
20	⌂ Tr	Tower	⊙ TOWER / ○ Tr	Tr ⊙		⌂	Tower
21	⌂	Water tower, Water tank on a tower	⊙ STANDPIPE / ○ S'pipe	⊙ WTR TR / ○ Wtr Tr		⌂	Water tower
22	⌂ Chy	Chimney	⊙ CHIMNEY / ○ Chy	⊙ CHY	⌂	⌂	Chimney
23	⌂	Flare stack (on land)	⊙ FLARE	○ Flare		⌂	Flare stack
24	⌂ Mon	Monument (including column, pillar, obelisk, statue, calvary cross)	⊙ MONUMENT / ○ Mon		⌂ ⌂	⌂	Monument
25.1	×	Windmill	⊙ WINDMILL / ○ Windmill	⊗	✱ ⚹	× ✦	Windmill, status of ruins is obtained by cursor pick
25.2	× Ru	Windmill (without sails)					
26.1	⌂ † ⚹	Wind turbine, Windmotor	⊙ WINDMOTOR / ○ Windmotor			⌂	Wind motor
26.2	(⌂) (⌂)	Onshore wind farm	⊙ WIND FARM / ○ Wind Farm			⊕	Wind generator farm
27	⌂ FS	Flagstaff, Flagpole	⊙ FS / ⊙ FP	○ FS / ○ FP		⌂	Flagstaff, flagpole
28	⌂	Radio mast, Television mast	⊙ R MAST / ⊙ TV MAST	○ R Mast / ○ TV Mast		⌂	Mast
29	⌂	Radio tower, Television tower	⊙ R TR / ⊙ TV TR	○ R Tr / ○ TV Tr		⌂	Radio, television tower
30.1	⊙ Radar Mast ⌂ Radar	Radar mast	⊙ RADAR MAST	○ Radar Mast		⌂	Mast
30.2	⊙ Radar Tr ⌂ Radar	Radar tower	⊙ RADAR TR	○ Radar Tr		⌂	Radar tower

Landmarks   E

No.	INT	Description	NOAA	NGA	Other NGA	ECDIS	
30.3	⊙ Radar Sc	Radar scanner				🗼	Radar scanner
30.4	⊙ Radome	Radome	⊙ DOME (RADAR) / ○ Dome (Radar)	⊙ RADOME / ○ Radome		⌒	Dome
31	📡	Dish aerial	⊙ ANT (RADAR) / ○ Ant (Radar)			📡	Dish aerial
32	⊕ ⊙ • Tanks	Tanks	⊙ TANK ⊕ ⊘ ○ Tk			○	Tank
						🛢	Tank farm
33	○ Silo ⊙ Silo	Silo	⊙ SILO ○ Silo / ⊙ ELEVATOR ○ Elevator		⚱ ⚱	●	Silo
34.1	(fortified symbol)	Fortified structure (on large scale charts)	(symbol) (symbol)			(symbol)	Fortified structure
34.2	⊞	Castle, Fort, Blockhouse (on small scale charts)			⊞	□	Fortified structure
34.3	⊞	Battery, Small fort (on small scale charts)					
35.1	(quarry symbol)	Quarry (on large scale charts)				⊗	Quarry area
35.2	⚒	Quarry (on small scale charts)				⚒	Quarry
36	⚒	Mine					
37.1	🚐	Recreational vehicle site					
37.2	⛺	Camping site (including recreational vehicles)					
Supplementary National Symbols							
a		Muslim shrine	† ☪				
b		Tomb	† ⚰				
c		Watermill	† ⚙		✶		

31

E   Landmarks

No.	INT	Description	NOAA	NGA	Other NGA	ECDIS
d		Factory	▨ ▮ ⌐ Facty			
e		Well	o Well			
f		School	■ Sch	⚑ Sch		
g		Hospital	■ Hosp			
h		University	■ Univ	⚑ Univ		
i		Gable	⊙ GAB	o Gab		
k		Telegraph Telegraph office	Tel Tel Off			
l		Magazine	Magz			
m		Government house	Govt Ho			
n		Institute	Inst			
o		Courthouse	Ct Ho			
p		Pavilion	Pav			
q		Telephone	T			
r		Limited	Ltd			
s		Apartment	Apt			
t		Capitol	Cap			
u		Company	Co			
v		Corporation	Corp			

Ports F

No.	INT	Description	NOAA	NGA	Other NGA	ECDIS	
Protective Structures						Supplementary national symbols: a–c	
1		Dike, Levee, Berm					Dike as a line
							Dike as a line, conspicuous
							Dike as an area
2.1		Seawall (on large scale charts)					Seawall
2.2		Seawall (on small scale charts)					
3		Causeway					Causeway as a line
							Causeway, covers and uncovers as a line
							Causeway as an area
							Causeway, covers and uncovers as an area
4.1		Breakwater (in general)					Breakwater as a line
4.2		Breakwater (loose boulders, tetrapods, etc.)					Breakwater as an area
4.3		Breakwater (slope of concrete or masonry)					
5		Training wall (partly submerged at high water)					Training wall

33

F Ports

No.	INT	Description	NOAA	NGA	Other NGA	ECDIS	
6		Groin (partly submerged at high water)	Groin				Groin (intertidal)

Harbor Installations

Depths → I   Anchorages, Limits → N   Beacons and other fixed marks → Q   Marina → U

No.	INT	Description	NOAA	NGA	Other NGA	ECDIS	
10		Fishing harbor					Fishing harbor
11.1		Boat harbor, Marina					Yacht harbor, marina
11.2		Yacht berths without facilities					
11.3		Yacht club, Sailing club					
12		Mole (with berthing facility)					Mole as a line / Mole as an area
13		Quay, Wharf	Whf				Wharf (quay)
14		Pier, Jetty	Pier				Pier (jetty), promenade pier
15		Promenade pier					
16		Pontoon					Pontoon as a line / Pontoon as an area
17		Landing for boats	Lndg				Landing

34

Ports F

No.	INT	Description	NOAA	NGA	Other NGA	ECDIS	
18		Steps, Landing stairs			Steps		Landing steps
19.1	④ Ⓑ Ⓐ 54	Designation of berth	3	A 3		Nr 3	Berth number
19.2	Ⓥ	Visitors' berth					Yacht harbor, marina
19.3		Dangerous cargo berth					
20	⬡ □Dn □Dns	Dolphin	o Dol † ● Dol (Great Lakes)				Mooring dolphin
21		Deviation dolphin					Deviation mooring dolphin
22	.	Minor post or pile	o Pile † ● Pile (Great Lakes)			●	Pile or bollard
23		Slipway, Patent slip, Ramp					Slipway, ramp
24		Gridiron, Scrubbing grid, Careening grid					Gridiron
25		Dry dock, Graving dock					Dry dock
26		Floating dock					Floating dock as a line / Floating dock as an area
27	7.6m	Non-tidal basin, Wet dock					Wet dock and gate

35

F   Ports

No.	INT	Description	NOAA	NGA	Other NGA	ECDIS
28		Tidal basin, Tidal harbor				Dock / Dock, under construction or ruined
29.1	Log Pond / Floating Barrier	Floating barrier, e.g. security, containment booms (ice, logs, oil), shark nets: - with supports - without supports				Floating hazard / Boom / Floating oil barrier, oil retention (high pressure pipe) / Boom, floating obstruction
29.2	Bubble Curtain	Bubble curtain (bubbler, pneumatic pipe)				Floating oil barrier, oil retention (high pressure pipe)
30	Dock under construction (2011)	Works on land, with year date				
31	Area under reclamation (2011)	Works at sea, Area under reclamation, with year date	Under construction (2011)	Under constr		Ruin or works under construction. Year and condition of under construction or ruin is obtained by cursor pick
32	Under construction (2011) / Works in progress (2011)	Works under construction, with year date	Under constr (2011)			
33.1	Ru	Ruin	Ruins			
33.2	Pier (ru)	Ruined pier, partly submerged at high water	Pier			Pier, ruined and partly submerged
34	Hulk / Hulk	Hulk	Hk	Hk		Hulk

Ports F

No.	INT	Description	NOAA	NGA	Other NGA	ECDIS	
Canals, Barrages						Supplementary national symbol: d	
Cultural Features → B Clearances → D Signal Stations → T							
40		Canal	Canal / Ditch				Canal
41.1		Lock (on large scale charts)					Lock gate as a line / Lock gate as an area
41.2		Lock (on small scale charts)	Canal / Lock / Ditch / Sluice (Tidegate, Floodgate)				Navigable lock gate
42		Gate, Caisson					Non-navigable lock gate / Caisson as a line / Caisson as an area
43		Flood barrage					Non-navigable lock gate / Flood barrage as a line / Flood barrage as an area
44		Dam, Weir (direction of flow shown is left to right)					Dam as a line / Dam as an area

F Ports

No.	INT	Description	NOAA	NGA	Other NGA	ECDIS	
Transhipment Facilities						Supplementary national symbols: e–f	
Roads → D Railways → D Tanks → E							
50	RoRo	Roll-on, Roll-off Ferry Terminal (RoRo Terminal)				RoRo	RoRo terminal
51		Transit shed, Warehouse (with designation)				■	Conspicuous single building, designation is obtained by cursor pick
52	#	Timber yard				#	Timber yard as a point
						⌐#¬	Timber yard as an area
53.1	(3t)	Crane with lifting capacity, Traveling crane (on railway)					Lifting capacity is obtained by cursor pick
						⊤	Crane as a point
						▮	Crane as an area
53.2	(50 t)	Container crane (with lifting capacity)		Crane Crane			
						▮	Crane, visually conspicuous as an area
Public Buildings						Supplementary national symbol: g	
60	⚓	Harbormaster's office	Hbr Mr			■	Conspicuous single building
61	⊖	Custom office	■ Cus Ho			■	Conspicuous single building
						⊖	Customs
62.1	⊕	Health office, Quarantine building	†	⊕ Health Office		■	Conspicuous single building
62.2	⊕ Hospital	Hospital	■ Hosp				
63	† ✉	Post office	■ PO				

Ports F

No.	INT	Description	NOAA	NGA	Other NGA	ECDIS
Supplementary National Symbols						
a		Jetty (partly below MHW)				
b		Submerged jetty				
c		Jetty (on small scale charts)				
d		Pump-out facilities				
e		Quarantine office				
g		Conveyor				

H   Tides, Currents

Terms Relating to Tide Levels

INT Terms		
No.	Term	Description
1	CD	Chart Datum, Datum for sounding reduction
2	LAT	Lowest Astronomical Tide
3	HAT	Highest Astronomical Tide
4	MLW	Mean Low Water
5	MHW	Mean High Water
6	MSL	Mean Sea Level
8	MLWS	Mean Low Water Springs
9	MHWS	Mean High Water Springs
10	MLWN	Mean Low Water Neaps
11	MHWN	Mean High Water Neaps
12	MLLW	Mean Lower Low Water
13	MHHW	Mean Higher High Water
14	MHLW	Mean Higher Low Water
15	MLHW	Mean Lower High Water
16	Sp	Spring tide
17	Np	Neap tide

Supplementary National Terms (see l–t for other terms and symbols)		
No.	Term	Description
a	HW	High Water
b	HHW	Higher High Water
c	LW	Low Water
d	LWD	Low Water Datum
e	LLW	Lower Low Water
f	MTL	Mean Tide Level
g	ISLW	Indian Spring Low Water
h	HWF&C	High Water Full and Change (Vulgar establishment of the port)
i	LWF&C	Low Water Full and Change
j	CRD	Columbia River Datum
k	GCLWD	Gulf Coast Low Water Datum

Tides, Currents H

No.	
	Tidal Levels and Charted Data
	Tide Gauge → T
20	Planes of reference are not exactly as shown below for all charts. They are usually defined in notes under chart titles. *Diagram labels:* Spot height 128; Topographic contours; 100; Overhead power cable; Safe vertical clearance (magenta); Charted vertical clearance; Elevation of light source; Charted coastline (HW or MSL); MHHW; MHW; (7) Islet height; MSL; Sea surface at any time; Height of tide; Observed depth; (12) Drying height; MLW; Charted LW (drying) line; MLLW (Chart datum); Charted depth (sounding) Notes: 1) The numbers *128, 100, (7)* and (12), shown above, are examples of how spot heights, topographic contour labels, islet heights and drying heights appear on NOAA paper charts. The numbers are enclosed in (parentheses) if the value is offset into the water to more clearly show the islet or rock. 2) On NOAA charts, except for lake charts, the HW (coast) line is equal to the MHW line.
	Tide Tables

No.	INT	Description	NOAA
30	**Tidal Levels referred to datum of soundings** 	Place	Lat N	Long E	Heights in metres above datum				 	---	---	---	---	---	---	---
			MHWS	MHWN	MLWN	MLWS
Norderney, Riffgat	53°42′	7°09′	3.2	2.8	0.9	0.4
Langeoog	53°43′	7°30′	3.4	3.0	0.9	0.4
			MHHW	MLHW	MHLW	MLLW
								Tabular statement of semi-diurnal or diurnal tides Note: The order of the columns of levels will be the same as that used in national tables of tidal predictions.	**TIDAL INFORMATION** | PLACE || Height referred to datum of soundings (MLLW)		
---	---	---	---	---
NAME	(LAT/LONG)	Mean Higher High Water	Mean High Water	Mean Low Water
		feet	feet	feet
Baltimore, Ft. McHenry	(39°16′N/76°35′W)	1.7	1.4	0.2
Annapolis, U.S. Naval Academy	(38°59′N/76°29′W)	1.4	1.2	0.2
Washington D.C., Washington Channel	(38°52′N/77°01′W)	3.2	2.9	0.1	 Dashes (---) located in datum columns indicate unavailable datum values for a tide station. Real-time water levels, tide predictions, and tidal current predictions are available on the Internet from http://tidesandcurrents.noaa.gov. (Nov 2011)

H   Tides, Currents

No.	INT		ECDIS	
31	Tidal stream table	Tidal streams referred to... Hours / Geographical Position / A 53°51.2'N 7°17.8'E. Before High Water 6–1, After High Water 1–6. Directions of streams (degrees), Rates at spring tides (knots), Rates at neap tides (knots). Values: -6 261 0.8 0.7; -5 170 0.2 0.1; -4 097 1.1 0.8; -3 095 1.5 1.2; -2 094 1.3 1.1; -1 092 1.0 0.9; 0 081 0.7 0.6; +1 038 0.3 0.2; +2 291 0.6 0.4; +3 277 1.0 0.8; +4 270 1.2 1.0; +5 267 1.1 1.0; +6 264 1.0 0.9	◇	Point or area for which a tidal stream table is available
			◇ (within dashed boundary)	Boundary of an area for which there is tidal information

Tidal Streams and Currents

Supplementary national symbols: m–t

Breakers → K   Tide Gauge → T

No.	INT	Description	NOAA	NGA	Other NGA	ECDIS	
40	→3.0 kn→	Flood tide stream with mean spring rate				↑ 2.5 kn	Flood stream, rate at spring tides
						? ↑ ?	Current or tidal stream whose direction is not known
						(dashed boundary)	Boundary of an area for which there is tidal information
41	→2.8 kn→	Ebb tide stream with mean spring rate				↑ 2.5 kn	Ebb stream, rate at spring tides
						? ↑ ?	Current or tidal stream whose direction is not known
						(dashed boundary)	Boundary of an area for which there is tidal information

Tides, Currents   H

No.	INT	Description	NOAA	NGA	Other NGA	ECDIS	
42	►►►►→	Current in restricted waters				↑ 2.5 kn	Non-tidal current
43	2.5 – 4.5 kn ∿∿∿→ Jan – Mar (see Note)	Ocean current with rates and seasons		∿∿∿→	∿∿∿→ (see Note)		
44	≈≈ ≈≈≈ ≈≈ ≈≈	Overfalls, tide rips, races	*Tide rips* ∧∧∧ ≈≈≈ ∧∧∧∧ symbol used only in small areas	≈≈		∾∾∾ ∾∾∾ ⸺ (∾∾∾)	Overfalls, tide rips; eddies; breakers as point, line, and area
45	⟲ ⟲ ⟲ ⟲ ⟲ ⟲	Eddies	⟲ ⟲ ⟲ *Eddies* ⟲ ⟲ ⟲ symbol used only in small areas				
46	Ⓐ	Position of tabulated tidal stream data with designation				◇	Point for which a tidal stream table is available
47	[a]	Offshore position for which tidal levels are tabulated					
Supplementary National Symbols (Supplementary national terms relating to tidal levels are listed after H 17)							
l		Stream	Str				
m		Current, general, with rate	►►►→ 2 kn				
n		Velocity, Rate	vel				
o		Knots	kn				
p		Height	ht				
q		Flood	fl				
u		Gulf Stream Limits	→ → → → → *Approximate location of Axis of Gulf Stream*				

I Depths

No.	INT	Description	NOAA	NGA	Other NGA	ECDIS	
General							
1	ED	Existence doubtful				25	Sounding of low accuracy
2	SD	Sounding of doubtful depth				25	Sounding of low accuracy
						212	Underwater hazard with depth greater than 20 meters
						✖	Isolated danger of depth less than the safety contour
3.1	Rep	Reported, but not confirmed				25	Sounding of low accuracy
						?	Point feature or area of low accuracy
3.2	Rep (2011)	Reported (with year of report), but not confirmed				▫ ▫ ▫ ▫	Low accuracy line demarking area wreck or obstruction
						▫ ▫ ▫ ▫	Low accuracy line demarking foul area
4	184 212	Reported, but not confirmed sounding or danger (on small scale charts only)				●	Obstruction, depth not stated
						25	Sounding of low accuracy
						5	Underwater hazard with depth of 20 meters or less
						212	Underwater hazard with depth greater than 20 meters
						✖	Isolated danger of depth less than the safety contour
						?	Point feature or area of low accuracy

Depths I

No.	INT	Description	NOAA	NGA	Other NGA	ECDIS	
Soundings						Supplementary national symbols: a–c	
Plane of Reference for Depths → H		Plane of Reference for Heights → H					
10	12 9_7	Sounding in true position (NOAA shows fathoms and feet with vertical numbers and meters with sloping numbers)	12 3_2 $2\frac{1}{2}$			9_7	Sounding shoaler than or equal to safety depth
						30	Sounding deeper than safety depth
11	. (4_8) | +(12) | 3375	Sounding out of position	(23) 3375			Depths are always shown in their true position in ECDIS	
12	(4_7)	Least depth in narrow channel	(4_7)				
13	$\overline{200}$	No bottom found at depth shown				200	Status of no bottom found is obtained by cursor pick
14	12 9_7	Soundings which are unreliable or taken from a smaller scale source (NOAA shows unreliable soundings in fathoms and feet with sloping numbers and in meters with vertical numbers)				12	Sounding of low accuracy
15		Drying heights and contours above chart datum				4	Drying height, less than or equal to safety depth
16		Natural watercourse (in intertidal area)					Tideway

45

I Depths

No.	INT	Description	NOAA	NGA	Other NGA	ECDIS
Depths in Fairways and Areas						Supplementary national symbols: a, b
Plane of Reference for Depths → H						
20	------------	Limit of dredged area	------------			Dredged area Depth, date of latest survey and other information is obtained by cursor pick
21	7.0 m 3.5 m	Dredged channel or area with minimum depth regularly maintained				
22	12m (2011) Dredged to 7.2m (2011)	Dredged channel or area with depth and year of the latest control survey	30 FEET APR 2011 30 FEET APR 2011			
24	10₈ 10₂ 9₆ (2011) 11 9₈	Area swept by wire drag. The depth is shown at chart datum. (The latest date of sweeping is shown in parentheses.)	3 29 23 8 22 30 18 7 21	7₆ (1930)		swept to 9.6 Swept area
25	Unsurveyed (see ZOC Diagram) Depths (see Note) Inadequately surveyed Unsurveyed	Unsurveyed or inadequately surveyed area; area with inadequate depth information	Unsurveyed 13 11 12 13 10 17 rky 22 20		Unsurveyed (see Note) Depths (see Note) Unsurveyed (see Note) Depths (see Note)	Incompletely surveyed area Unsurveyed area

ECDIS Portrayal of Depths

ECDIS depth related symbols closely resemble their paper chart counterparts; however, ECDIS provides valuable additional information to mariners that paper charts cannot.

Soundings

ECDIS enables mariners to set their own-ship "safety depth." If no depth is set, ECDIS sets the value to 30m. Soundings equal to or shoaler than the safety depth are shown in black; deeper soundings are displayed in a less conspicuous gray. Fractional values are shown with subscript numbers of the same size.

Depth Contours & Depth Areas

Depth contours in ECDIS are portrayed with a thin gray line. Each pair of adjacent depth contours is used to create depth area features. These are used by ECDIS to tint different depth levels and to initiate alarms when a ship is headed into unsafe water.

Depth Contour Labels

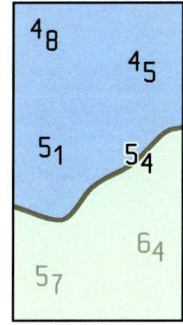

ECDIS depth contour labels are not centered and oriented along isolines as they appear on paper charts. They are displayed upright and may appear either on or next to the contour lines that they describe. The labels are black and the same size as soundings, but the labels have a light "halo" to set them apart. The graphic to the left shows depth labels and soundings both deeper and shoaler than the safety depth. Note that depths on NOAA paper charts and ENCs are usually compiled in fathoms and feet. Because ECDIS displays depths in meters, soundings and contour lines often show fractional meter values. The "own-ship safety contour" (described below) is always displayed, but mariners may choose to have all other depth contours turned off.

Safety Contour

ECDIS uses a "safety contour" value to show an extra thick line for the depth contour that separates "safe water" from shoaler areas. If the mariner does not set an own-ship safety contour value, ECDIS sets the value to 30m. If the ENC being displayed does not have a contour line equal to the safety contour depth value set by the mariner, then ECDIS sets the next deeper contour as the safety contour. Depending on the contour intervals used on individual ENCs, ECDIS may set different safety contours as a ship transits from one ENC to another. ECDIS will initiate an alarm if the ship's future track will cross the safety contour within a specified time set by the mariner.

Two or Four Tints for Shading Depth Areas

ECDIS tints all depth areas beyond the (green tinted) foreshore in either one of two or one of four shades of blue. This is similar to the convention used for paper charts, but the depths used to change from one tint to another are based on the safety contour and thus "customized" for each ship. If the mariner chooses two shades to be displayed, water deeper than the safety contour is shown in an off-white color, water shoaler than the safety contour is tinted blue.

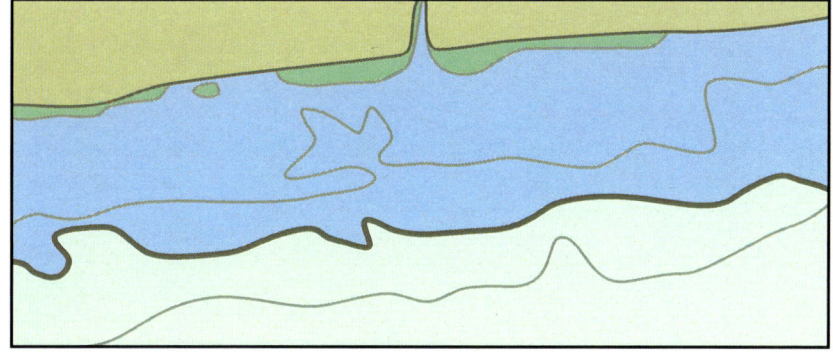

Portrayal of Depth Areas with 2 Color Settings

Some ECDIS enable mariners to define two additional depth areas for medium-deep water and medium-shallow water by setting a "deep contour" value and a "shallow contour" value. If this option is used, the safety contour is displayed between the medium deep and medium shallow contours.

Portrayal of Depth Areas with 4 Color Setting

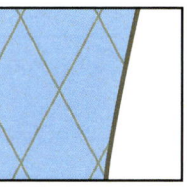

Some ECDIS also provide the mariner with the option of displaying a cross-hatch "shallow water" pattern over all depth areas shoaler than the safety contour.

I Depths

No.	INT	Description	NOAA	NGA	Other NGA	ECDIS
Depth Contours						
30	(depth contour scale: 2, 0, 2, 3, 5, 8, 10, 15, 20, 25, 30, 40, 50, 75, 100, 200, 300, 400, 500, 600, 700, 800, 900, 1000, 2000, 3000, 4000, 5000, 6000, 7000, 8000, 9000, 10000)	Drying contour Low water line Blue tint, in one or more shades, or tint ribbons are shown to different limits according to the scale and purpose of the chart and the nature of the bathymetry. On some charts, contours and values are printed in blue.	(depth contour scale: 1–10000)			Two Shades / Four Shades: foreshore, shallow depth / very shallow depth, shallow water contour / medium shallow depth, safety contour, deep depth / medium deep depth, deep water contour, all deeper contours / deep depth
31	— — 20 — — / — — 50 — —	Approximate depth contours	— — 20 — — / — — 50 — —			▫ ▫ ▫ ▫ Approximate depth contour ▫ ▫ ▫ ▫ Approximate safety depth contour
Supplementary National Symbols						
a		Swept channel	(swept channel with depth 6)			
b		Swept area, not adequately sounded (shown by purple or green tint)	(area with 89, 15, 102, 10, 119)			
c		Stream	(stream with 2ft, 5, 6)			

Nature of the Seabed   J

No.	INT	Description	NOAA	NGA	Other NGA	ECDIS	
Types of Seabed						Supplementary national abbreviations: a–ag	
Rocks → K							
1	S	Sand				S	Sand
2	M	Mud				M	Mud
3	Cy	Clay				Cy	Clay
4	Si	Silt				Si	Silt
5	St	Stones				St	Stones
6	G	Gravel				G	Gravel
7	P	Pebbles				P	Pebbles
8	Cb	Cobbles				Cb	Cobbles
9.1	R	Rock; Rocky	Rk; rky			R	Rock
9.2	Bo	Boulder(s)	Blds			R	Boulder
						R	Lava
10	Co	Coral, Coralline algae				Co	Coral
11	Sh	Shells (skeletal remains)				Sh	Shells
12.1	S/M	Two layers, e.g. sand over mud					
12.2	fS M Sh fS.M.Sh	The main constituent is given first for mixtures, e.g. fine sand with mud and shells	f S M Sh				
13.1	Wd	Weed (including kelp)					Weed, kelp
13.2	*(symbol)*	Kelp, Weed	*(symbol)* Kelp			*(symbol)*	Weed, kelp as an area
13.3	Sg	Seagrass					

J Nature of the Seabed

No.	INT	Description	NOAA	NGA	Other NGA	ECDIS	
14	(wavy line)	Sandwaves	Sandwaves		(wavy line)	(sand wave symbols)	Sand waves as a point / Sand waves as a line / Sand waves as an area
15	T	Spring in seabed	Spring			T	Spring

Types of Seabed, Intertidal Areas

No.	INT	Description	NOAA	NGA	Other NGA	ECDIS	
20	(G, St area)	Area with stones and gravel	Gravel			gravel / stone	Areas of gravel and stone
21	(S, 1₂, (4₂))	Rocky area, which covers and uncovers		Rock	(rock shapes)	(rocky area)	Rocky ledges or coral reef
22	(S, (1₆), (4₂))	Coral reef, which covers and uncovers	Coral		(coral shapes)		

Qualifying Terms

Supplementary national symbols: ah–bf

No.	INT	Description	NOAA	NGA	Other NGA	ECDIS	
30	f	Fine	only used in relation to sand				
31	m	Medium					
32	c	Coarse					
33	bk	Broken					
34	sy	Sticky					
35	so	Soft					
36	sf	Stiff					
37	v	Volcanic	vol				
38	ca	Calcareous	Ca			(calcareous area)	Rocky ledges or coral reef
39	h	Hard					

Nature of the Seabed   J

No.	INT	Description	NOAA	NGA	Other NGA	ECDIS
Supplementary National Abbreviations						
a		Ground		*Grd*		
b		Ooze		*Oz*		
c		Marl		*Ml*		
d		Shingle		*Sn*		
f		Chalk		*Ck*		
g		Quartz		*Qz*		
h		Schist		*Sch*		
i		Coral head		*Co Hd*		
j		Madrepores		*Mds*		
k		Volcanic ash		*Vol Ash*		
l		Lava		*La*		
m		Pumice		*Pm*		
n		Tufa		*T*		
o		Scoriae		*Sc*		
p		Cinders		*Cn*		
q		Manganese		*Mn*		
r		Oysters		*Oys*		
s		Mussels		*Ms*		
t		Sponge		*Spg*		
u		Kelp		*K*		
v		Grass		*Grs*		
w		Sea-tangle		*Stg*		
x		Spicules		*Spi*		
y		Foraminifera		*Fr*		
z		Globigerina		*Gl*		
aa		Diatoms		*Di*		
ab		Radiolaria		*Rd*		
ac		Pteropods		*Pt*		
ad		Polyzoa		*Po*		
ae		Cirripedia		*Cir*		
af		Fucus		*Fu*		

J   Nature of the Seabed

No.	INT	Description	NOAA	NGA	Other NGA	ECDIS
ag		Mattes		*Ma*		
ah		Small		*sml*		
ai		Large		*lrg*		
aj		Rotten		*rt*		
ak		Streaky		*str*		
al		Speckled		*spk*		
am		Gritty		*gty*		
an		Decayed		*dec*		
ao		Flinty		*fly*		
ap		Glacial		*glac*		
aq		Tenacious		*ten*		
ar		White		*wh*		
as		Black		*bl; bk*		
at		Violet		*vi*		
au		Blue		*bu*		
av		Green		*gn*		
aw		Yellow		*yl*		
ax		Orange		*or*		
ay		Red		*rd*		
az		Brown		*br*		
ba		Chocolate		*ch*		
bb		Gray		*gy*		
bc		Light		*lt*		
bd		Dark		*dk*		
be		Varied		*vard*		
bf		Uneven		*unev*		

Rocks, Wrecks, Obstructions and Aquaculture   K

No.	INT	Description	NOAA	NGA	Other NGA	ECDIS	
General							
1		Danger line: A danger line draws attention to a danger which would not stand out clearly enough if represented solely by its symbol (e.g. isolated rock) or delimits an area containing numerous dangers, through which it is unsafe to navigate					Obstruction, depth not stated
							Obstruction which covers and uncovers
							Underwater hazard with depth of 20 meters or less
							Isolated danger of depth less than the safety contour
							Foul area, not safe for navigation
2	7_5	Depth swept by wire drag or confirmed by diver (This symbol may be combined with other symbols, e.g. wrecks, obstructions, wells.)	21 Rk 35 Rk 4_6 Obstn 4_6 Wk	4_6 Obstn 4_6 Wk (1937)	# (15_7)	4 21	Swept sounding, less than or equal to safety depth / Swept sounding, greater than safety depth
3	20	Safe clearance depth. The exact depth is unknown, but is estimated to have a safe clearance at the depth shown	4_6 Wk 35 Rk	4_6 Obstn			ECDIS displays safe clearance depths in the same manner as known depths.
Rocks							
Plane of Reference for Heights → H		Plane of Reference for Depths → H					
10	(4,1) (3,1) (1,7)	Rock (islet) which does not cover, height above height datum	25 (21)		▲ (4 m)	O 8 m	Land as a point at small scale / Land as an area, with an elevation or control point
11	3_7 2_7 (1_6) (1_6)	Rock which covers and uncovers, height above chart datum	*(2) (2) 4	(0_6) Uncov 1m (0_6) Uncov 1m		✱ 4 ✕	Rock which covers and uncovers or is awash at low water / Underwater hazard which covers and uncovers with drying height / Isolated danger of depth less than the safety contour

K   Rocks, Wrecks Obstructions and Aquaculture

No.	INT	Description	NOAA	NGA	Other NGA	ECDIS	
12		Rock awash at the level of chart datum			⊛	✳	Rock which covers and uncovers or is awash at low water
						● (green)	Underwater hazard which covers and uncovers
						⊗	Isolated danger of depth less than the safety contour
13		Underwater rock of unknown depth, dangerous to surface navigation				⊕	Dangerous underwater rock of uncertain depth
						⊗	Isolated danger of depth less than the safety contour
14		Underwater rock of known depth					
14.1		inside the corresponding depth area	12 *Rk*	27 *Rk* 21 *R*		5	Underwater hazard with a depth of 20 meters or less
						25	Underwater hazard with depth greater than 20 meters
14.2		outside the corresponding depth area, dangerous to surface navigation	(5) *Rk*	(4) *Rk* (5) *R*		⊗	Isolated danger of depth less than the safety contour
15	35 *R*	Underwater rock of known depth, not dangerous to surface navigation	35*Rk*		35 *R.* +(35)	10	Underwater hazard with a depth of 20 meters or less
						25	Underwater hazard with depth greater than 20 meters

Rocks, Wrecks, Obstructions and Aquaculture K

No.	INT	Description	NOAA	NGA	Other NGA	ECDIS	
16	(coral reef symbol with +Co +Co)	Coral Reef which is always covered	(+Co 3₁ reef line diagrams)			(symbols)	Dangerous underwater rock of uncertain depth
							Obstruction, depth not stated
							Isolated danger of depth less than the safety contour
							Safe clearance shoaler than safety contour
						12_8	Safe clearance deeper than safety contour
						25_6	Safe clearance deeper than 20 meters
17	(breaker symbols) 5_8 Br, 19, 18	Breakers	Breakers (symbol)	Br (symbol)	West Breaker PA	(wave symbols)	Overfalls, tide rips; eddies; breakwaters as point, line, and area

Wrecks and Fouls

Plane of Reference for Depths → H

No.	INT	Description	NOAA	NGA	Other NGA	ECDIS	
20	Mast (1.2) Wk	Wreck, hull never covers, on large scale charts, height above height datum	Hk	Hk		○ 1.2 m	Wreck, always dry, with height shown
21	Mast (1₂) Wk	Wreck, covers and uncovers, on large scale charts, height above chart datum	Hk		Wk, Wk, Wk, Wk	1_2	Wreck, covers and uncovers
						(oval with dashes)	Distributed remains of wreck

K Rocks, Wrecks Obstructions and Aquaculture

No.	INT	Description	NOAA	NGA	Other NGA	ECDIS	
22	Wk Wk	Submerged wreck, depth known, on large scale charts			Wk	5₂	Submerged wreck with depth of 20 meters or less
						25	Submerged wreck with depth greater than 20 meters
							Distributed remains of wreck
23	Wk	Submerged wreck, depth unknown, on large scale charts		Hk	Wk / Wk / Wk	⊗	Submerged wreck with depth less than the safety contour or depth unknown
24		Wreck showing any portion of hull or superstructure at level of chart datum			Wk / Wk / Wk / Wk		Wreck showing any portion of hull or superstructure at level of chart datum
25	Masts	Wreck of which the mast(s) only are visible at chart datum	Masts	Mast (10ft) Funnel			
26	4₆ Wk 25 Wk	Wreck, least depth known by sounding only			(11)	5	Underwater hazard with depth of 20 meters or less
						25	Underwater hazard with depth greater than 20 meters
						⊗	Isolated danger of depth less than the safety contour
27	4₆ Wk 25 Wk	Wreck, depth swept by wire drag or confirmed by diver	25 Wk			4₆	Swept sounding for underwater hazard less than safety depth
						25	Swept sounding for underwater hazard greater than or equal to safety depth
						⊗	Isolated danger of depth less than the safety contour

Rocks, Wrecks, Obstructions and Aquaculture K

No.	INT	Description	NOAA	NGA	Other NGA	ECDIS	
28	⊕	Dangerous wreck, depth unknown				⊞ (blue)	Dangerous wreck, depth unknown
						⊗ (magenta)	Isolated danger of depth less than the safety contour
29	+++	Sunken wreck, not dangerous to surface navigation				+++	Non-dangerous wreck, depth unknown
30	(25) Wk	Wreck over which the exact depth is unknown, but which is estimated to have a safe clearance at the depth shown.			(4) Wk	5 (blue)	Underwater hazard with safe clearance of 20 meters or less
						25	Underwater hazard with safe clearance greater than 20 meters
						⊗ (magenta)	Isolated danger of depth less than the safety contour
31.1	#	Foul ground, not dangerous to surface navigation, but to be avoided by vessels anchoring, trawling, etc. (e.g. remains of wreck, cleared platform)				#	Foul area of seabed safe for navigation but not for anchoring
31.2	#----#----# [#]					(ellipse with #)	Foul ground
						(ellipse with X X X)	Distributed remains of wreck

Obstructions and Aquaculture

Plane of Reference for Depths → H   Kelp, Seaweed → J   Underwater Installations → L

No.	INT	Description	NOAA	NGA	Other NGA	ECDIS	
40	Obstn ◌ Obstn	Obstruction, depth unknown				◌ (blue dotted)	Obstruction, depth not stated
						⊗ (magenta)	Isolated danger of depth less than the safety contour
						X ⊗ X X (blue area)	Safe clearance shoaler than safety contour

57

K   Rocks, Wrecks Obstructions and Aquaculture

No.	INT	Description	NOAA	NGA	Other NGA	ECDIS	
41	4₆ Obstn 16₈ Obstn	Obstruction, least depth known by sounding only				5	Underwater hazard with depth of 20 meters or less
						25	Underwater hazard with depth greater than 20 meters
						⊗	Isolated danger of depth less than the safety contour
42	4₆ Obstn 16₈ Obstn	Obstruction, depth swept by wire drag or confirmed by diver				4	Less than or equal to safety depth (swept depth)
						21	Greater than safety depth (swept depth)
							Method of depth measurement is obtained by cursor pick
						5 ✻	Underwater hazard with depth of 20 meters or less (known by diver or other means)
						25 ✻	Underwater hazard with depth greater than 20 meters
						⊗	Isolated danger of depth less than the safety contour
43.1	⊤ ⊤ ⊤ ○ Obstn	Stumps of posts or piles, wholly submerged	○ ○ Subm piles	○ Piles	⊤ ⊤	●	Obstruction, depth not stated
						5	Underwater hazard with depth of 20 meters or less
43.2	⊤	Submerged pile, stake, snag, or stump (with exact position)	○ Subm piles ○ Stakes ○ Snags	○ Well ○ Deadhead ○ Stump	⊤ ⊤ ⊤	⊗	Isolated danger of depth less than the safety contour
44.1	⊥⊥⊥ ⊥⊥⊥	Fishing stakes	⊥⊥⊥⊥⊥ Fsh stks			⊥⊥⊥	Fish stakes as a point
						(area symbol)	Fish stakes as an area
44.2	(fish trap symbol)	Fish trap, Fish weir, Tunny nets	Fish trap □			(symbol)	Fish trap, fish weir, tunny net as a point

Rocks, Wrecks, Obstructions and Aquaculture — K

No.	INT	Description	NOAA	NGA	Other NGA	ECDIS	
45	Fish traps / Tunny nets	Fish trap area, Tunny nets area	(purple dashed boundary)			(area with symbols)	Fish trap, fish weir, tunny net as an area
46.1	(fish symbols in area)	Fish haven	Obstn Fish Haven	(actual shape)		⊗	Isolated danger of depth less than the safety contour
						⊗ (hatched blue)	Safe clearance shoaler than safety contour
46.2	(fish symbols with 2_4, (2_4))	Fish haven with minimum depth	Obstn Fish Haven (auth min 42ft)			5	Underwater hazard with depth of 20 meters or less
						25	Underwater hazard with depth greater than 20 meters
						⊗	Isolated danger of depth less than the safety contour
						⊗ (hatched blue)	Safe clearance shoaler than safety contour
						12_8	Safe clearance deeper than safety contour
						25_6	Safe clearance deeper than 20 meters
47	(shellfish symbols)	Shellfish beds					
48.1	(marine farm symbols, area)	Marine farm (on large scale charts), area of marine farms		Marine Farm		(marine farm point symbol)	Marine farm as a point
48.2	(marine farm symbols)	Marine farm (on small scale charts)		Obstn (Marine Farm) / Marine Farm		(area with symbols)	Marine farm as an area

Supplementary National Symbols

No.	INT	Description	NOAA	NGA	Other NGA	ECDIS	
a		Rock which covers and uncovers, (height unknown)	* ⊛				

K   Rocks, Wrecks Obstructions and Aquaculture

No.	INT	Description	NOAA	NGA	Other NGA	ECDIS
b		Shoal sounding on isolated rock or rocks	⑤ Rk ㉑ Rks		⑨ R ② r ② P ⊕ (8)	
c		Sunken wreck covered 20 to 30 meters	⊞		⊞	
d		Submarine volcano		( ) Sub vol		
e		Discolored water		( ) Discol water		
f		Sunken danger, least depth cleared by wire drag	21 Rk 4₆	35 Rk 4₆ Obstn		
g		Reef of unknown extent		Reef		
h		Coral reef, detached (uncovers at sounding datum)	✳ Co 🪨	Co Coral ✳ Co Co		
i		Submerged crib	[ ] Subm Crib	[ ] Crib		
j		Crib, duck blind (above water)	■ Duck Blind ▢ Crib			
k		Submerged duck blind	[ ] Duck Blind			
l		Submerged platform	[ ] Subm platform	[ ] Platform		
m		Coral reef which covers and uncovers		Hay Reef 2₂		
n		Sinkers		Sinkers 13₄ 14₆ 15₇		
o		Foul area, foul with rocks or wreckage, dangerous to navigation	Foul Wks Wreckage			
p		Unexploded ordnance	( ) Unexploded Ordnance	( ) Unexploded Ordnance		
q		Float	□ Float			
r		Stumps of posts or piles, which cover and uncover	∘∘ Subm piles			

Offshore Installations   L

No.	INT	Description	NOAA	NGA	Other NGA	ECDIS	
General							
Areas, Limits → N							
1	*Ekofisk Oilfield*	Name of oilfield or gasfield		CORRIB GAS FIELD (with Wells 3348, 3346, 3334, 3344)			Area to be navigated with caution, name is obtained by cursor pick
2	Z-44	Platform with designation/name		"Name"			Offshore platform, name is obtained by cursor pick
3		Limit of safety zone around offshore installation					Area where entry is prohibited or restricted or to be avoided, with other cautions
4		Limit of development area					Cautionary area, navigate with caution
5.1		Wind turbine, floating wind turbine, vertical clearance under blade			Fl.Y		Wind motor visually conspicuous
5.2		Offshore wind farm					Wind farm (offshore)
		Offshore wind farm (floating)					
6		Wave farm, Renewable energy device					Wave farm
Platforms and Moorings							
Mooring Buoys → Q							
10		Production platform, Platform, Oil derrick	■	▫			Offshore platform
11	Fla	Flare stack (at sea)					Conspicuous flare stack on offshore platform

61

L Offshore Installations

No.	INT	Description	NOAA	NGA	Other NGA	ECDIS	
12	SPM	Single Point Mooring (SPM), including Single Anchor Leg Mooring (SALM), Articulated Loading Column (ALC)		"Name"			Offshore platform, name and status of disused is obtained by cursor pick
14	Ru Z-44 (ru)	Disused platform with superstructure removed			(disused)		
16		Single Buoy Mooring (SBM), Oil or gas installation buoy including Catenary Anchor Leg Mooring (CALM)					Installation buoy and mooring buoy, simplified
							Installation buoy, paper chart
17		Moored storage tanker, Accommodation vessel		Tanker			Offshore platform
18	————→)	Mooring ground tackle				—————⊥	Ground tackle

Underwater Installations

Supplementary national symbol: a

Plane of Reference for Depths → H   Obstructions → K

No.	INT	Description	NOAA	NGA	Other NGA	ECDIS	
20	Well	Submerged production well	Well (cov 21ft) Well (cov 83ft)	Well	Prod Well Prod Well	5	Underwater hazard with depth of 20 meters or less
						25	Underwater hazard with depth greater than 20 meters
						⊗	Isolated danger of depth less than the safety contour
21.1	Well	Suspended well, depth over wellhead unknown	Pipe			⊗	Isolated danger of depth less than the safety contour
21.2	4_3 Well 15 Well	Suspended well, with depth over wellhead	Pipe (cov 24ft) Pipe (cov 92ft)			5	Underwater hazard with depth of 20 meters or less
						25	Underwater hazard with depth greater than 20 meters
						⊗	Isolated danger of depth less than the safety contour

Offshore Installations L

No.	INT	Description	NOAA	NGA	Other NGA	ECDIS	
22	#	Site of cleared platform				#	Foul area of seabed safe for navigation but not for anchoring
23	★ ○ Pipe ⊙ Pipe (1₈)	Above-water wellhead (lit or unlit)	○ Pipe		⊙ Pipe (2₄)	▪	Obstruction in the water which is always above water level
24	○ Turbine ★ Fl(2) Underwater Turbine	Underwater turbine				(symbol with i)	Underwater turbine or subsurface ODAS
25	○ ODAS	Subsurface Ocean(ographic) Data Acquisition System (ODAS)				(symbol with i)	

Submarine Cables

No.	INT	Description	NOAA	NGA	Other NGA	ECDIS	
30.1	～～～～	Submarine cable				～～～	Submarine cable
30.2	┬┬┬～～～┬┬┬ ┴┴┴～～～┴┴┴	Submarine cable area	† Cable Area			(bordered area)	Submarine cable area
31.1	～～〰～～	Submarine power cable					
31.2	┬┬┬〰┬┬┬ ┴┴┴〰┴┴┴	Submarine power cable area					
32	～ ～ ～ ～	Disused submarine cable				～～～✴	Status of disused is obtained by cursor pick

Submarine Pipelines

No.	INT	Description	NOAA	NGA	Other NGA	ECDIS	
40.1	Oil Gas (see Note) Chem Water	Supply pipeline: unspecified, oil, gas, chemicals, water				(pipeline crossing land/water)	Oil, gas pipeline, submerged or on land
40.2	Oil Gas (see Note) Chem Water	Supply pipeline area: unspecified, oil, gas, chemicals, water	† Pipeline Area		(area diagram)	(bordered area with i)	Submarine pipeline area with potentially dangerous contents

L Offshore Installations

No.	INT	Description	NOAA	NGA	Other NGA	ECDIS	
41.1	Water, Sewer, Outfall, Intake	Outfall and intake: unspecified, water, sewer, outfall, intake					Water pipeline, sewer, etc.
41.2	Water, Sewer, Outfall, Intake	Outfall and intake area: unspecified, water, sewer, outfall, intake	Pipeline Area				Submarine pipeline area with generally non-dangerous contents
42.1	Buried 1.6m	Buried pipeline/pipe (with nominal depth to which buried)					Nominal depth of buried pipeline is obtained by cursor pick
42.2		Pipeline tunnel					Pipeline tunnel
43	Obstn	Diffuser, Crib					Underwater hazard with depth of 20 meters or less; Isolated danger of depth less than the safety contour
44		Disused pipeline/pipe					Status of disused is obtained by cursor pick
Supplementary National Symbols							
a		Submerged well (buoyed)	Well Well	Well			
b		Potable water intake	PWI Depth over Crib 17 ft	Crib			

Tracks, Routes M

No.	INT	Description	NOAA	NGA	Other NGA	ECDIS
Tracks						Supplementary national symbols: a–c
Tracks Marked by Lights → P		Leading Beacons → Q				
1	270.5° / 2 Bns ǂ 270.5°	Leading line (solid line is the track to be followed, ǂ means "in line")		Lights in line 090°		Leading line bearing a non-regulated, recommended track — -<?>- Direction not encoded; 270 deg One-way; 270 deg Two-way
2	270.5° / Island open of Headland 270.5°	Transit (other than leading line), clearing line		Beacons in line 090°	Bns in line 270.5°	270 deg Clearing line; transit line
3	090.5°–270.5°	Recommended track based on a system of fixed marks		Lights in line 090°	-->-->-- / -->-->--	Non-regulated, recommended track based on fixed marks — -<?>- Direction not encoded; 90 deg One-way; 270 deg Two-way
4	090.5°–270.5°	Recommended track not based on a system of fixed marks		--<-->-- / --<-->--		Non-regulated, recommended track not based on fixed marks — -<?>- Direction not encoded; 90 deg One-way; 270 deg Two-way
5.1	(symbols) DW (see Note)	One-way track and DW track based on a system of fixed marks		-->-->--		Based on fixed marks, one-way; 90 deg Non-regulated recommended track; DW Deep water route
5.2	270° / DW	One-way track and DW track not based on a system of fixed marks				Not based on fixed marks, one-way; 90 deg Non-regulated recommended track; DW Deep water route centerline
6	<7.0m> / <7.3m>	Recommended track with maximum authorized (or recommended) draft stated		<7 m> / <7₃ m>		If encoded, the shoalest depth range value along the track is obtained by cursor pick

65

M Tracks, Routes

No.	INT	Description	NOAA	NGA	Other NGA	ECDIS	
Routing Measures						Supplementary national symbols: d–e	
Basic Symbols							
10		Established (mandatory) direction of traffic flow					Traffic direction in a one-way lane of a traffic separation scheme
11		Recommended direction of traffic flow					Single traffic direction in a two-way route part of a traffic-separation scheme
12		Separation line (large scale, small scale)					Traffic separation line
13		Separation zone					Traffic separation zone
14		Limit of restricted routing measure (e.g. Inshore Traffic Zone (ITZ), Area to be Avoided (ATBA))	RESTRICTED AREA				
15		Limit of routing measure					Traffic separation scheme boundary
16		Precautionary area					Traffic precautionary area as a point / Traffic precautionary area as an area
17		Archipelagic Sea Lane (ASL); axis line and limit beyond which vessels shall not navigate					Axis and boundary of archipelagic sea lane
18		Fairway designated by regulatory authority: with minimum depth / with maximum authorized draft (may be highlighted by gray tint)	SAFETY FAIRWAY 166.200 (see note A)				Fairway, depth is obtained by cursor pick

Tracks, Routes   M

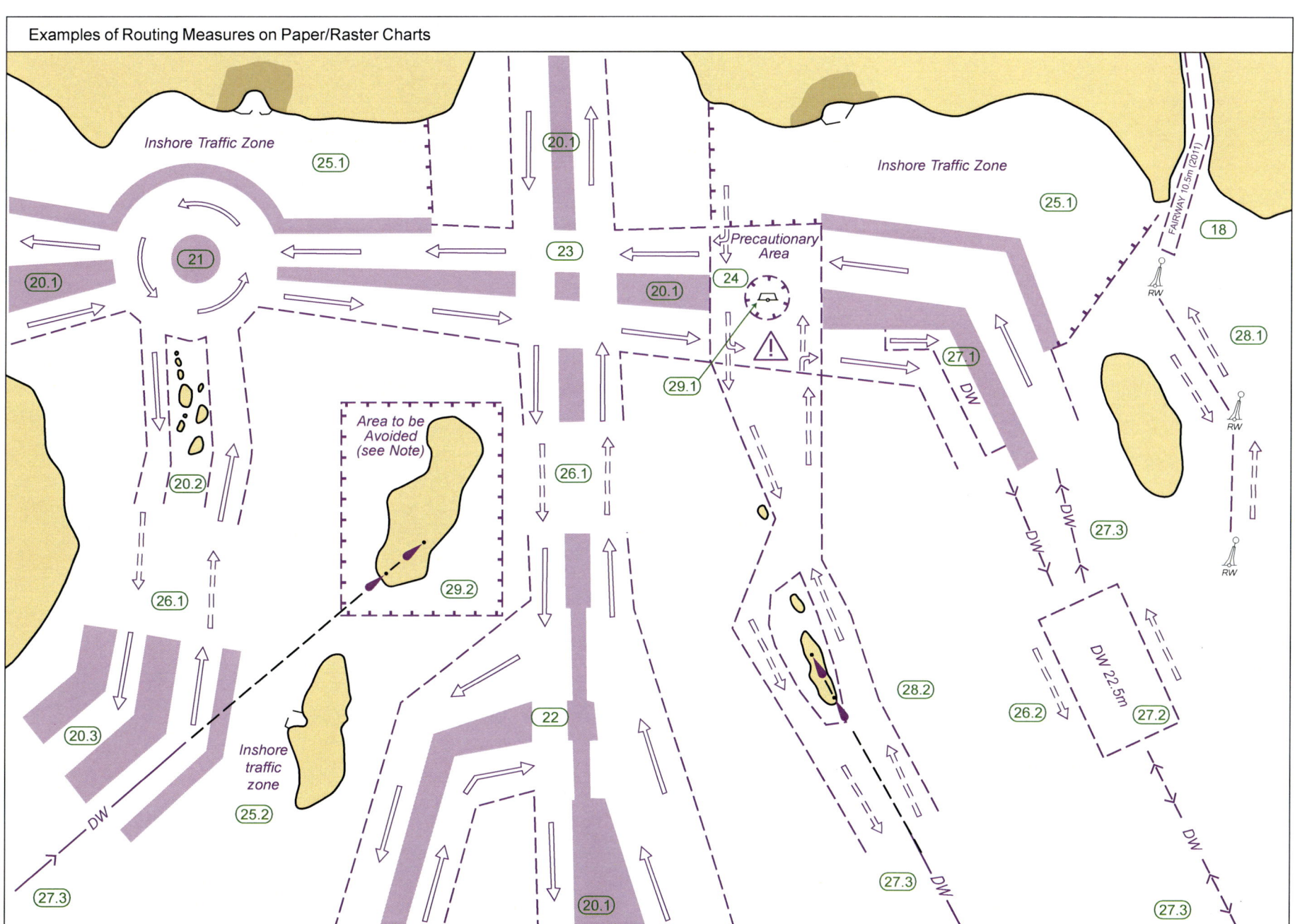

Examples of Routing Measures on Paper/Raster Charts

M Tracks, Routes

No.	
Examples of Routing Measures	
18	Safety fairway
20.1	Traffic Separation Scheme (TSS), traffic separated by separation zone
20.2	Traffic Separation Scheme, traffic separated by natural obstructions
20.3	Traffic Separation Scheme, with outer separation zone separating traffic using scheme from traffic not using it
21	Traffic Separation Scheme, roundabout with separation zone
22	Traffic Separation Scheme, with "crossing gates"
23	Traffic Separation Scheme crossing, without designated precautionary area
24	Precautionary area
25.1	Inshore Traffic Zone (ITZ), with defined end limits
25.2	Inshore Traffic Zone, without defined end limits
26.1	Recommended direction of traffic flow, between traffic separation schemes
26.2	Recommended direction of traffic flow, for ships not needing a deep water route
27.1	Deep water route (DW), as part of one-way traffic lane
27.2	Two-way deep water route, with minimum depth stated
27.3	Deep water route, centerline as recommended one-way or two-way track
28.1	Recommended route, one-way and two-way (often marked by centerline buoys)
28.2	Two-way route, with one-way sections
29.1	Area to be Avoided (ATBA), around navigational aid
29.2	Area to be Avoided, e.g. because of danger of stranding

Tracks, Routes M

Examples of Routing Measures in ECDIS

M   Tracks, Routes

No.	INT	Description	NOAA	NGA	Other NGA	ECDIS	
Radar Surveillance Systems							
30	Radar Surveillance Station	Radar surveillance station	⊙ Ra			◉	Radar station
31	Ra Cuxhaven	Radar range					Radar range
32.1	────── Ra ──────	Radar reference line			—Ra——Ra—	270 deg (dashed)	Radar line
32.2	Ra 090°–270°	Radar reference line coinciding with a leading line				—<?>— — — <	Non-regulated recommended track based on fixed marks; Direction not encoded
						→ 90 deg →	One-way
						← 270 deg →	Two-way
Radio Reporting Points							
40.1	⊲◯ Ⓑ ⑦ VHF 80	Radio reporting (calling-in or way) points showing direction(s) of vessel movement with designation (if any) and VHF-channel				△ Nr 13 ch 74	Radio calling-in point for traffic in one direction only
						◇ Nr 13 ch 74	Radio calling-in point for traffic in both directions
						? ◇ ? Nr 13 ch 74	Radio calling-in point, direction not encoded
40.2	– – – ◇ – – –	Radio reporting line				– – △ – – Nr 13 ch 74	Radio calling-in point for traffic in one direction only
						– – ◇ – – Nr 13 ch 74	Radio calling-in point for traffic in both directions
						– ? ◇ ? – Nr 13 ch 74	Radio calling-in point, direction not encoded

Tracks, Routes   M

No.	INT	Description	NOAA	NGA	Other NGA	ECDIS
Ferries						
50	----------▭----------	Ferry	(Ferry illustration)			—▭ — — — ⊏ Ferry route
51	----------▭---------- Cable Ferry	Cable Ferry	Cable Ferry			—▭ — — — ⊏ Cable ferry route
Supplementary National Symbols						
a		Recommended track for deep draft vessels (track not defined by fixed marks)	←—DW—→			
b		Depth is shown where it has been obtained by the cognizant authority	←——DW 83ft	←——DW 76ft		
c		Alternate course	----------			

N   Areas, Limits

No.	INT	Description	NOAA	NGA	Other NGA	ECDIS
General *						
Dredged and Swept Areas → I Submarine Cables, Submarine Pipelines → L Tracks, Routes → M						
On multi-colored charts, symbols in Section N may be in green when associated with environmental areas.						
1.1	Tint band may vary in width between 1–5 mm	Maritime limit in general usually implying permanent physical obstructions (tint band for emphasis)				Caution area, a specific caution note applies
1.2		usually implying no permanent physical obstructions (tint band for emphasis)				
2.1		Limit of restricted area (tint band for emphasis)	RESTRICTED AREA			Area where entry is prohibited or restricted or to be avoided
2.2		Limit of area into which entry is prohibited	PROHIBITED AREA PROHIBITED AREA			Area where entry is prohibited or restricted or to be avoided, with other cautions Area where entry is prohibited or restricted or to be avoided, with other information
Anchorages, Anchorage Areas						
10	⚓	Reported anchorage (no defined limits)			⚓ ⚓	⚓ Anchorage area as a point at small scale, or anchor points of mooring trot at large scale
11.1	⚓(A) ⚓(E 53) ⚓(14)	Anchor berths	14		6 ⚓ No 1	⚓ Nr 6 Anchor berth
11.2	(⚓(A)) (⚓(E 53)) (⚓(14))	Anchor berths with swinging circle	○ D-17	D17		Radius of swing circle is obtained by cursor pick

* ECDIS represents many types of area limits with just a few different symbols. Information about the type of area and its associated restrictions or prohibitions may be obtained by cursor pick.

Areas, Limits   N

No.	INT	Description	NOAA	NGA	Other NGA	ECDIS	
12.1	(anchorage area symbol with anchor)	Anchorage area in general	(dashed line)	Anchorage (with anchor)			
12.2	No 1 ⚓	Numbered anchorage area	ANCH NO 1 110.000 (see note A)	Anchorage No. 1			
12.3	Name ⚓	Named anchorage area	SOUTH ANCH 110.000 (see note A)	Neufeld Anchorage			
12.4	DW ⚓	Deep water anchorage area, Anchorage area for deep draft vessels		DW Anchorage		(anchorage symbol with cursor)	Type of anchorage area is obtained by cursor pick
12.5	Tanker ⚓	Tanker anchorage area		Tanker Anchorage			
12.6	24 h ⚓	Anchorage area for periods up to 24 hours					
12.7	(symbol) ⚓	Dangerous cargo anchorage area	EXPLOSIVES ANCHORAGE				
12.8	⊕⚓	Quarantine anchorage area	QUAR ANCH / QUARANTINE ANCHORAGE	Quarantine Anchorage			
12.9	Reserved ⚓ (see Note)	Reserved anchorage area					

Note: Anchors as part of the limit symbol are not shown for small areas. Other types of anchorage areas may be shown.

| 13 | (seaplane symbols) | Seaplane operating area | SEAPLANE LANDING AREA | | | (seaplane landing symbol) | Seaplane landing area |
| 14 | (seaplane) ⚓ | Anchorage for seaplanes | | | | (anchorage symbol with cursor) | Type of anchorage area is obtained by cursor pick |

73

N   Areas, Limits

No.	INT	Description	NOAA	NGA	Other NGA	ECDIS	
Restricted Areas						Supplementary national symbols: d, e, g	
On multi-colored charts, the magenta symbols may be in green when associated with environmental areas.							
20		Anchoring prohibited	ANCH PROHIBITED	ANCH PROHIB			Area where anchoring is prohibited or restricted
							Area where anchoring is prohibited or restricted, with other cautions
							Area where anchoring is prohibited or restricted, with other information
21.1		Fishing prohibited	FISH PROHIBITED	FISH PROHIB			Area where fishing or trawling is prohibited or restricted
							Area where fishing or trawling is prohibited or restricted, with other cautions
							Area where fishing or trawling is prohibited or restricted, with other information

Areas, Limits N

No.	INT	Description	NOAA	NGA	Other NGA	ECDIS	
21.2		Diving prohibited					Area where diving is prohibited
22		Environmentally Sensitive Sea Areas					Environmentally Sensitive Sea Area (ESSA)
		Bird sanctuary					
		Seal sanctuary					Area with minor restrictions or information notices
	Note: Other animal silhouettes (e.g. seahorses, penguin, petrel) may be used, as appropriate.						
		Non-specific nature reserve, National parks, Marine Reserves (MR)					
		Particularly Sensitive Sea Area (PSSA)					PSSA
	Tint band may vary in width between 1–5 mm						

75

N Areas, Limits

No.	INT		Description	NOAA	NGA	Other NGA	ECDIS	
23.1	Explosives Dumping Ground	(symbol)	Explosives dumping ground, individual mine or explosive	EXPLOSIVES DUMPING AREA			(i symbol)	Explosives or chemical dumping ground as a point
23.2	Explosives Dumping Ground (disused)		Explosives dumping ground (disused), Foul (explosives)	EXPLOSIVES DUMPING AREA DISUSED			(i area symbol)	Explosives or chemical dumping ground as an area
24	Dumping Ground for Chemicals		Dumping ground for chemical waste	Dump Site	Dumping Ground			
25	Degaussing Range		Degaussing range (DG range)	DEGAUSSING RANGE	DEGAUSSING RANGE		(− symbol)	Degaussing area
27	5kn		Maximum speed				(cursor)	If a speed restriction exists, the speed limit is obtained by cursor pick

Military Practice Areas

No.	INT	Description	NOAA	NGA	Other NGA	ECDIS	
30	(symbol)	Firing practice area				(! symbol)	Restricted area
31	Entry Prohibited	Military restricted area, entry prohibited	PROHIBITED AREA	Prohibited Area		(− symbol)	Area where entry is prohibited or restricted or to be avoided, with other cautions
32	(symbol)	Mine-laying (and counter-measures) practice area				(! symbol)	Restricted area
33	(submarine symbol)	Submarine transit lane and exercise area			SUBMARINE EXERCISE AREA		
34	Minefield (see note)	Minefield				(− symbol)	Minefield

International Boundaries and National Limits

Supplementary national symbols: a, f, h

No.	INT	Description	NOAA	NGA	Other NGA	ECDIS	
40	CANADA ++++++++ UNITED STATES	International boundary on land				T T T T T T	Jurisdiction boundary

Areas, Limits   N

No.	INT	Description	NOAA	NGA	Other NGA	ECDIS	
41	CANADA / UNITED STATES	International maritime boundary					Jurisdiction boundary
42		Straight territorial sea baseline with base point					Straight territorial sea baseline
43		Seaward limit of territorial sea			TERRITORIAL SEA		Territorial sea
44		Seaward limit of contiguous zone					Contiguous zone
45		Limits of fishery zones					Limits of fishery zone
46	Continental Shelf	Limit of continental shelf					Continental shelf area
47	EEZ	Limit of Exclusive Economic Zone (EEZ)					Exclusive economic zone
48		Customs limit					Custom regulations zone
49	Harbor Limit	Harbor limit		Harbor Limit			Harbor area, symbolized

Various Limits

Supplementary national symbols: a, b

No.	INT	Description	NOAA	NGA	Other NGA	ECDIS	
60.1	(2012)	Limit of fast ice, Ice front (with date)					Continuous pattern for an ice area (glacier, etc.)
60.2	(2012)	Limit of sea ice (pack ice) seasonal (with date)					
62.1	Spoil Ground	Spoil ground	Spoil Area				HO information note
62.2	Spoil Ground (disused)	Spoil ground (disused)	Spoil Area Discontinued				
63	Extraction Area	Extraction (dredging) area					Dredging area
64	Cargo Transhipment Area	Cargo transhipment area					HO information note
65 †	Incineration Area	Incineration area					

N   Areas, Limits

No.	INT	Description	NOAA	NGA	Other NGA	ECDIS
Supplementary National Symbols						
a		COLREGS demarcation line	– – – – – – –			
b		Limit of fishing area (fish trap areas)	— — — —			
c		Dumping ground	Dumping Ground			
d		Dumping area (Dump site)	Disposal Area 92 Depths from survey of 2010 85			
f		Reservation line (Options)				
g		Dump site	Dump Site			
h		Three Nautical Mile Line	THREE NAUTICAL MILE LINE			
i		No Discharge Zone	NO-DISCHARGE ZONE			

Lights   P

No.	INT	Description	NOAA	NGA	Other NGA	ECDIS	
\multicolumn{8}{l}{Light Structures and Major Floating Lights}
\multicolumn{8}{l}{Minor Light Floats → Q30, 31}
1.1	☆ ★ Lt LtHo	Position of navigation light (size and style of "star" may vary) light, lighthouse	•		☆ ◇ ● •		Light, lighthouse, paper chart
1.2		Light on standard charts	•				
1.3	☆ (yellow circle)	Significant all-round light, generally for offshore navigation on multicolored charts					
2.1		Lighted offshore platform on standard charts	■ PLATFORM (lighted)				Lighted offshore platform, paper chart
2.2		Lighted offshore platform on multicolored charts					
3	BY ☆BnTr	Lighted beacon tower	○ Marker (lighted)				Lighted beacon tower, paper chart
4	R BRB ☆Bn	Lighted beacon					Lighted beacon, paper chart
5	R ☆Bn	Articulated light, buoyant beacon, resilient beacon	○ Art				
\multicolumn{8}{l}{Note: Minor lights, fixed and floating, usually conform to IALA Maritime Buoyage System characteristics.}
7		Navigational lights on landmarks or other structures					
8	Holnis Iso.W.6s32m13M 310° 320°	Important light off chart limits					

79

P Lights

No.	Abbreviaton INT	Abbreviaton NOAA	Class of Light	Illustration Period Shown		ECDIS
Light Characters						
Light Characters on Light Buoys → Q						
10.1	F	F	Fixed		F	
	Occulting (total duration of light longer than total duration of darkness)					
10.2	Oc	Oc	Single-occulting		Oc	
	Oc(2) Example	Oc (2)	Group-occulting		Oc (2)	
	Oc(2+3) Example	Oc (2+3)	Composite group-occulting		Oc (2+3)	
10.3	Isophase (duration of light and darkness equal)					
	Iso	Iso	Isophase		Iso	
	Flashing (total duration of light shorter than total duration of darkness)					
10.4	Fl	Fl	Single-flashing		Fl	When text for lights is displayed, ECDIS uses INT abbreviations.
	Fl(3) Example	Fl (3)	Group-flashing		Fl (3)	
	Fl(2+1) Example	Fl (2+1)	Composite group-flashing		Fl (2+1)	
10.5	LFl	L Fl	Long-flashing (flash 2s or longer)		L FL	
	Quick (repetition rate of 50 to 79 - usually either 50 or 60 - flashes per minute)					
10.6	Q	Q	Continuous quick		Q	
	Q(3) Example	Q (3)	Group quick		Q(3)	
	IQ	IQ	Interrupted quick		IQ	

Lights P

No.	Abbreviation INT	Abbreviation NOAA	Class of Light	Illustration / Period Shown		ECDIS
	\multicolumn{5}{l}{Very quick (repetition rate of 80 to 159 - usually either 100 or 120 - flashes per minute)}		
10.7	VQ	VQ	Continuous very quick		VQ	When text for lights is displayed, ECDIS uses INT abbreviations.
	VQ(3) Example	VQ (3)	Group very quick		VQ(3)	
	IVQ	IVQ	Interrupted very quick			
	\multicolumn{5}{l}{Ultra quick (repetition rate of 160 or more - usually 240 to 300 - flashes per minute)}		
10.8	UQ	UQ	Continuous ultra quick			
	IUQ	IUQ	Interrupted ultra quick			
10.9	Mo(K) Example	Mo (K)	Morse code		Mo (K)	
10.10	FFl	F Fl	Fixed and flashing		F Fl	
10.11	Al.WR	AlWR	Alternating	W R W R W R	Al WR	

P Lights

No.	INT		Description	NOAA	NGA	Other NGA	ECDIS
Colors of Lights							
11.1	W		White (for lights, only on sector and alternating lights)	Colors of lights shown on standard charts			Default light symbol if no color is encoded or color is other than red, green, white, yellow, amber, or orange
11.2	R		Red				Red
11.3	G		Green				
11.4	Bu		Blue	on multicolored charts			Green
11.5	Vi		Violet				
11.6	Y		Yellow				White, yellow, amber or orange
11.7	Y	Or	Orange	on multicolored charts at sector lights			
11.8	Y	Am	Amber				Sector lights
Period							
12	2.5s	90s	Period in seconds and tenths of a second				When text for lights is displayed, ECDIS uses INT abbreviations.
Elevation							
Plane of reference for Heights → H Tidal Levels → H							
13	12m		Elevation of light given in meters or feet	36ft			
Range							
14	15M		Light with single range				
14	15/10M		Light with two different ranges	10M only lesser of two ranges is charted		15/10M	
14	15-7M		Light with three or more ranges	7M only least of three ranges is charted			
Note: Charted ranges are nominal ranges given in Nautical Miles.							
Disposition							
15	(hor)		Horizontally disposed				
15	(vert)		Vertically disposed				Disposition of light is obtained by cursor pick
15	(∆)	(∇)	3 lights disposed in the shape of a triangle				

Lights   P

No.	INT	Description	NOAA	NGA	Other NGA	ECDIS
Example of a Full Light Description						
16	INT Example Name ☆ Fl(3)WRG.15s 21m 15-11M		NOAA Example Name • Fl (3) WRG 15s 21ft 11M	NGA Example Name • Fl (3) WRG 15s 21m 15-11M		FlR15s21m11M The descriptions of non-sector lights are shown in ECDIS when the display of text is turned on, as shown above. (The aid to navigation or other structure that is always shown attached to a light flare in ECDIS is not depicted here.) Sector lights (as described in the INT, NOAA and NGA examples at left) are depicted graphically in ECDIS, as shown below and in P40. The description of a sector light or any other type of light may always be obtained by cursor pick.
	Fl(3)	Class of light: group flashing repeating a group of three flashes	Fl(3)	Class of light: group flashing repeating a group of three flashes		
	WRG	Colors: white, red, green, exhibiting the different colors in defined sections	WRG	Colors: white, red, green, exhibiting the different colors in defined sections		
	15s	Period: the time taken to exhibit one full sequence of three flashes and eclipses: 15 seconds	15s	Period: the time taken to exhibit one full sequence of three flashes and eclipses: 15 seconds		
	21m	Elevation of focal plane above datum: 21 meters	21ft 21m	Elevation of light: 21 feet 21 meters		
	15-11M	Nominal range: white 15M, green 11M, red between 15 and 11M	11M 15-11M	Nominal range: shortest range of all the lights is 11M white 15M, green 11M, red between 15 and 11M		
Lights Marking Fairways						
Leading Lights and Lights in Line						
20.1	Name Oc.3s 8m 12M Name Oc.6s 24m 15M (Oc. 6s / Oc. 3s / 225.3°)	Leading lights with leading line (solid line is the track to be followed) and arcs of visibility on standard charts Bearing given in degrees and tenths of a degree	205°			Leading lights with sectors 225.3 deg

83

P Lights

No.	INT	Description	NOAA	NGA	Other NGA	ECDIS	
20.2	[diagram: Name Oc.3s 8m12M; Name Oc.6s 24m15M with arcs of visibility 225.3°]	Leading lights with leading line (solid line is the track to be followed) and arcs of visibility on multi-colored charts Bearing given in degrees and tenths of a degree					
20.3	[diagram: Oc.4s 12M, Oc.R 4s 10M, Oc & Oc.R ≠ 269.3°]	Leading lights (≠ means lights in line) on standard charts Bearing given in degrees and tenths of a degree				[diagram: Oc OcR ← 270 deg]	Leading lights
20.4	[diagram: Oc.4s 12M, Oc.R 4s 10M, Oc & Oc.R ≠ 269.3°]	Leading lights (≠ means lights in line) on multi-colored charts Bearing given in degrees and tenths of a degree					
20.5	Ldg.Oc.W&R	Leading lights on small scale standard charts					
20.6	Ldg.Oc.W&R	Leading lights on small scale multi-colored charts					
21.1	[diagram: Fl.G, Fl.G 270°; 2Fl.R 270°]	Lights in line, marking the sides of a channel on standard charts				[diagram: FlG FlG 270 deg; 2FlR 270 deg]	Lights in line, marking the sides of a channel
21.2	[diagram: Fl.G, Fl.G 270°; 2Fl.R 270°]	Lights in line, marking the sides of a channel on multi-colored charts					
22	Rear Lt or Upper Lt	Rear or upper light					
23	Front Lt or Lower Lt	Front or lower light					

Lights   P

No.	INT	Description	NOAA	NGA	Other NGA	ECDIS
Direction Lights						
30.1	Fl(2)5s10m11M Dir 269°	Direction light with narrow sector and course to be followed, flanked by darkness or unintensified light				Directional light with sector — 269 deg
30.2	Oc.12s6M Dir 299° Dir 255.5° Fl(2)5s11M	Direction light on standard charts with course to be followed, sector(s) uncharted				Directional light without sector — 209 deg / 165.5 deg Fl(2)5s11M Oc12s6M
30.3	Dir WRG. 15-5M F.G / Al.WG / F.W.4s / Al.WR / F.R	Direction light with narrow fairway sector flanked by light sectors of different character on standard charts				Light, directional
30.4	Dir WRG. 15-5M F.G / Al.WG / Oc.W.4s / Al.WR / F.R	Direction light with narrow fairway sector flanked by light sectors of different character on multicolored charts				
31	▲ Dir 295°	Moiré effect light (day and night), arrows show when course alteration needed			▲ Dir 295°	FY 270 deg — Category of light as moiré effect is obtained by cursor pick

Quoted bearings are always from seaward.

P Lights

No.	INT	Description	NOAA	NGA	Other NGA	ECDIS	
Sector Lights							
40.1	Fl.WRG.4s 21m18-12M	Sector light on standard charts					Light, sector
40.2	Fl.WRG.4s 21m18-12M	Sector light on multicolored charts					
40.3	Fl.WRG.4s 21m18-12M	Sector light on standard charts. Sectors not charted					
40.4	Fl.WRG.4s 21m18-12M	Sector lights on multicolored charts. Sectors not charted					
41.1	Oc.WRG. 10-6M	Sector lights on standard charts, the white sector limits marking the sides of the fairway					
41.2	Oc.WRG. 10-6M	Sector lights on multicolored charts, the white sector limits marking the sides of the fairway					

Lights   P

No.	INT	Description	NOAA NGA	Other NGA	ECDIS
42.1	Fl(3)10s 62m 25M F.R.55m 12M	Main light visible all-round with red subsidiary light seen over danger			Light, danger
43.1	Fl.5s 41m 30M	All-round light with obscured sector			Light, obscured
44.1	Iso.WRG	Light with arc of visibility deliberately restricted			Light, restricted

P   Lights

No.	INT	Description	NOAA	NGA	Other NGA	ECDIS	
45.1	Q.14m5M (Faint sector)	Light with faint sector					Light, faint
46.1	Oc.R.8s 7M (R.Intens); Oc.R.8s (R.5M, R.9M, R.5M)	Light with intensified sector					Intensified light visibility is obtained by cursor pick / Light, intensified

Lights with Limited Times of Exhibition

No.	INT	Description	NOAA	NGA	Other NGA	ECDIS
50	F.R.(occas)	Lights exhibited only when specially needed (for fishing vessels, ferries) and some private lights	Occas	F R (occas)		Status and condition of light is obtained by cursor pick
51	Fl.10s 40m 27M (F.37m 11M Day)	Daytime light (charted only where the character shown by day differs from that shown at night)		F Bu 9m 6M (F by day)		
52	Name Q.WRG.5m 10-3M (Fl.5s Fog)	Fog light (exhibited only in fog, or character changes in fog)				
53	† Fl.5s (U)	Unwatched (unmanned) light with no standby or emergency arrangements				
54	(temp)	Temporary				
55	(exting)	Extinguished				
56	(man)	Manually activated				

Special Lights

Flare Stack (as sea) → L   Flare Stack (on land) → E   Signal Stations → T

No.	INT	Description	NOAA	NGA	Other NGA	ECDIS	
60	Aero Al.Fl.WG.7.5s 11M	Aero light (may be unreliable)	AERO	AERO Al WG 7.5s 108m 13M	AERO	AeroAlFlWG7.5s11M	Light

Lights   P

No.	INT	Description	NOAA	NGA	Other NGA	ECDIS	
61.1	Aero F.R.313m 11M RADIO MAST (353)	Air obstruction light of high intensity (e.g. on radio mast)		AERO F R 77m 11M		AeroFR313m11M	Conspicuous mast with light
61.2	(89) (R Lts)	Air obstruction light of low intensity (e.g. on radio mast)		TR (RLts)			
62	Fog Det Lt	Fog detector light					Category of light is obtained by cursor pick
63	(Illuminated)	Floodlit, floodlighting of a structure					Floodlight
64		Strip light					Strip light
On multicolored charts, P63 and P64 may be any appropriate color.							
65	(priv)	Private light other than one exhibited occasionally	Priv	F R (priv)	Priv maintd		Status of private is obtained by cursor pick
66	(sync)	Synchronized light					
Supplementary National Symbols							
a		Riprap surrounding light					
b		Short-Long Flashing			S-L Fl		
c		Group-Short Flashing			G-S Fl		
d		Fixed and Group Flashing			F Gp Fl		
e		Unmanned light-vessel; light float			FLOAT		
f		LANBY, superbuoy as navigational aid					

Simplified and Traditional Paper Chart Symbols

ECDIS can be set to display aids to navigation with either traditional paper chart or simplified symbols. The two symbol sets are shown below. Some ECDIS color fill the paper chart buoy shapes, but this is not required by IHO ECDIS portrayal specifications.

Floating Marks

Paper Chart	Simplified	Simplified Symbol Name
*		Cardinal buoy, north
*		Cardinal buoy, east
*		Cardinal buoy, south
*		Cardinal buoy, west
		Default symbol for buoy (used when no defining attributes have been encoded in the ENC)
*		Isolated danger buoy
		Conical lateral buoy, green
		Conical lateral buoy, red
		Can shape lateral buoy, green
		Can shape lateral buoy, red
		Installation buoy and mooring buoy
**		Safe water buoy
		Special purpose buoy, spherical or barrel shaped, or default symbol for special purpose buoy
		Special purpose TSS buoy marking the starboard side of the traffic lane
		Special purpose TSS buoy marking the port side of the traffic lane
		Special purpose ice buoy or spar or pillar shaped buoy
		Super-buoy ODAS & LANBY
		Light float
		Light vessel

Fixed Marks

Paper Chart	Simplified	Simplified Symbol Name
*		Cardinal beacon, north
*		Cardinal beacon, east
*		Cardinal beacon, south
*		Cardinal beacon, west
		Default symbol for a beacon (used when no defining attributes have been encoded in the ENC)
		Isolated danger beacon
		Major lateral beacon, red
		Major lateral beacon, green
		Minor lateral beacon, green
		Major safe water beacon
		Minor safe water beacon
		Major special purpose beacon
		Minor special purpose beacon

* Paper chart symbols display various buoy or beacon shape symbols in conjunction with the topmark. Simplified portrayal only displays the topmark.
** Several different paper chart symbols correspond to this simplified symbol.

Day Marks

Paper Chart	Simplified	Simplified Symbol Name
		Square or rectangular daymark
		Triangular daymark, point up
		Triangular daymark, point down
		Retro reflector

Buoys, Beacons Q

No.	INT	Description	NOAA	NGA	Other NGA	ECDIS	
Buoys and Beacons							
IALA Maritime Buoyage System, which includes Beacons → Q 130							
		Default buoy symbol if no other defining attribution is provided				⚓?	Default symbol for buoy, paper chart
						⊙?	Default symbol for buoy, simplified
		Default beacon symbol if no other defining attribution is provided				↡?	Default symbol for a beacon, paper chart
						▮?	Default symbol for a beacon, simplified
1	—○—	Position of buoy or beacon	○			ECDIS shows the position of buoys and beacons with a circle at the bottom of paper chart symbols. For simplified symbols, the position of the aid corresponds with the center of the symbol.	
Colors of Buoys and Beacon Topmarks						Supplementary national symbols: p	
Abbreviations for Colors → P							
2	▲ ▲ ▲ ▰ ↑ G B G G G	Green and black (symbols filled black)	♦G ♦ ▰ ↓				
3	♁ ▵ ♁ ✕ ▯ R R Y Y R	Single color other than green and black	♦R ◇ ▲ ↓				
4	♁ ▲ • BY GRG BRB	Multiple colors in horizontal bands, the color sequence is from top to bottom	♦RG ▰ ▲ ▲ ↓				
5	♁ ↑ ↑ RW RW RW	Multiple colors in vertical or diagonal stripes, the darker color is given first	♦ RW ♁ ▲ ↓				
6		Retroreflecting material					
Lighted Marks						Supplementary national symbols: p	
Marks with Fog Signals → R						Supplementary national symbols: p	
7	▲Fl.G ↑Fl.R G R	Lighted marks on standard charts	♦Fl G • Fl R	↑Fl R R			
8	♁Fl.R ♁Iso ↑Fl.G R RW G	Lighted marks on multicolored charts					
Note: On standard charts, the light flares of buoys and beacons are shown in magenta. On multicolored charts, the light flares are shown in the colors of the appropriate light							

Q Buoys, Beacons

No.	INT	Description	NOAA	NGA	Other NGA	ECDIS	
Topmarks and Radar Reflectors							
For Application of Topmarks within the IALA System → Q 130			For other topmarks (special purpose buoys and beacons) → Q				
9		IALA System buoy topmarks (beacon topmarks shown upright)				Paper chart symbols for topmarks (on the left, below) are always displayed above a buoy or beacon shape symbol, as in Q 10 and Q 11. Simplified symbols (on the right, below) for cardinal marks, isolated dangers and safe water consist of only the topmark without the buoy shape symbol. Simplified symbology for marks with any other type of topmark will display only the simplified buoy or beacon shape symbol without a topmark.	
						▲▲ / ◁◁	2 cones point upward
						▼▼ / ▽▽	2 cones point downward
						▲▼ / ◁▽	2 cones base to base
						▼▲ / ▽◁	2 cones point to point
						•• / ○○	2 spheres
						• / ⊙	Sphere
						▲	Cone point up
						▼	Cone point down
						▯	Cylinder, square, vertical rectangle
						✕	X-shape
						/	Flag or other shape
						▭	Board, horizontal rectangle
						◇	Cube point up
						✚	Upright cross over a circle
						⊤	T-shape
10	No2	Beacon with topmark, color, radar reflector and designation	■ G "3" Ra Ref			bn No 2	Beacon in general with topmark, paper chart

Buoys, Beacons Q

No.	INT	Description	NOAA	NGA	Other NGA	ECDIS	
11	No3	Buoy with topmark, color, radar reflector and designation	G N "3"	No 3		by No 3	Conical buoy with topmark, paper chart

Note: Radar reflectors on floating marks usually are not charted. ECDIS does not display radar reflectors on fixed or floating aids; this information is obtained by cursor pick.

Buoys

Shapes of Buoys

Features Common to Buoys and Beacons → Q 1–11

						Paper Chart	Simplified	
20		Conical buoy, nun buoy, ogival buoy	N					Conical buoy
21		Can buoy or cylindrical buoy	C					Can buoy
22		Spherical buoy	SP					Spherical buoy
23		Pillar buoy; Buoy with no distinctive shape	P					Pillar buoy
24		Spar buoy, spindle buoy	S					Spar buoy
25		Barrel buoy, tun buoy						Barrel buoy
26 †		Superbuoy						Super-buoy / Lanby, super-buoy / Super-buoy odas & lanby

Light Vessels and Minor Light Floats

30.1	Fl.G.3s Name	Light float on standard charts						Light float
30.2	Fl.G.3s Name	Light float on multi-colored charts						
31 †	Fl.10s	Light float not part of IALA System						Light float
32		Light vessel						Light vessel, paper chart

Q Buoys, Beacons

No.	INT	Description	NOAA	NGA	Other NGA	ECDIS	
Mooring Buoys							
Oil or Gas Installation Buoy → L							
40		Mooring buoys					Mooring buoy, can shape, paper chart
							Mooring buoy, barrel shape, paper chart
							Istallation buoy and mooring buoy, simplified
41.1	Fl.Y.2.5s	Lighted mooring buoy (example) on standard charts		Fl Y 2s			Mooring buoy with light flare, barrel shape, paper chart
41.2	Fl.Y.2,5s	Lighted mooring buoy (example) on multi-colored charts					
42		Trot, mooring buoys with ground tackle and berth numbers				Nr 1	Trot, mooring buoys with ground tackle and berth numbers
43		Mooring buoy with telephonic communication		Tel Tel Tel = telegraphic T T T = telephonic			Mooring buoy, can shape, paper chart
							Mooring buoy, barrel shape, paper chart
							Installation buoy and mooring buoy, simplified
44	Small Craft Moorings	Numerous moorings (example)	Numerous mooring buoys	(5 buoys) Moorings			Small-craft mooring area
45		Visitors' mooring					Availability of visitor mooring at marina is obtained by cursor pick

Buoys, Beacons   Q

No.	INT	Description	NOAA	NGA	Other NGA	ECDIS	
Special Purpose Buoys							
Note: Shapes of buoys are variable. Lateral or Cardinal buoys may be used in some situations.							
						🖱	Purpose of buoy and other information is obtained by cursor pick
Purpose of buoy may be shown by label.							
50	⚓ DZ	Firing danger area (Danger Zone) buoy				⚠	Conical buoy with topmark, paper chart
54	⚓ DG	Degaussing Range buoy				⊙	Special purpose buoy, spherical or barrel shaped, or default symbol for special purpose buoy, simplified
58	⛴ ODAS ⚓ ODAS	ODAS buoy (Ocean Data Acquisition System), data collecting buoy	⛴ ODAS	⛴ ODAS		⛴	Super-buoy, paper chart
						⛴	Super-buoy odas & lanby, simplified
						⌒	Spherical buoy, paper chart
						⊙	Spherical buoy, simplified

Q Buoys, Beacons

No.	INT	Description	NOAA	NGA	Other NGA	ECDIS
70	☼ (priv) Y	Buoy privately maintained (example)	◊ Priv		☼ (occas) Y ☼ (01.04.–31.10.) Y	Status as private is obtained by cursor pick
71	☼ (Apr–Oct) Y	Seasonal buoy (example)				Status as periodic and period start and stop dates are obtained by cursor pick

Beacons

Lighted Beacons → P   Features Common to Beacons and Buoys → Q1–11

No.	INT	Description	NOAA	NGA	Other NGA	ECDIS
80	↓ ⊙ Bn	Beacon in general, characteristics unknown or chart scale too small to show	□ Bn	★ Bn G ⊙ Bn R		Default symbol for a beacon, paper chart Default symbol for a beacon, simplified Beacon in general, paper chart
81	↓ BW	Beacon with color, no distinctive topmark	▲ R □ RW ■ G Bn			Beacon color is obtained by cursor pick
82	↓ R ↑ BY ↑ BRB	Beacons with colors and topmarks (examples)				Beacon color is obtained by cursor pick See note at Q 9 for information about topmarks and ECDIS simplified symbology Beacon in general with topmark, paper chart Major red lateral beacon, simplified Beacon in general with topmark, paper chart Cardinal beacon, north, simplified Beacon in general with topmark, paper chart Isolated danger beacon, simplified

Buoys, Beacons Q

No.	INT	Description	NOAA	NGA	Other NGA	ECDIS	
83	BRB	Beacon on submerged rock with colors (topmark as appropriate)		BRB			Beacon in general with topmark, paper chart
							Isolated danger beacon, simplified
Minor Impermanent Marks Usually in Drying Areas (Lateral Marks of Minor Channels)							
Minor Pile → F							
90		Stake, pole	† o Stake • Stake † o Pole • Pole	R			Minor, stake or pole beacon, paper chart
91	Port Hand / Starboard Hand	Perch, withy		R			Minor, stake or pole beacon, paper chart
							Minor red lateral beacon, simplified
92	† / †	Withy					Minor green lateral beacon, simplified
Minor Marks, Usually on Land							
Landmarks → E							
100		Cairn	o Cairn	⊙ CAIRN			Conspicuous cairn
101	☐ Mk	Colored or white mark					Square or rectangular day mark, paper chart
							Square or rectangular day mark, simplified
							Triangular day mark, point up, paper chart
							Triangular day mark, point up, simplified
							Triangular day mark, point down, paper chart
							Triangular day mark, point down, simplified

Q Buoys, Beacons

No.	INT	Description	NOAA	NGA	Other NGA	ECDIS	
102.1 †		Colored topmark (color known or unknown) with function of a beacon					
102.2 †		Painted boards with function of leading beacons					

Beacon Towers

110		Beacon towers without and with topmarks and colors (examples)	RW Bn				Beacon tower, paper chart
							Beacon tower with topmarks, paper chart
							Major red lateral beacon, simplified
							Major green lateral beacon, simplified
111		Lattice beacon					Lattice beacon, paper chart

Special Purpose Beacons

Leading Lines, Clearing Lines → M

Note: Topmarks and colors shown where scale permits.

120		Leading beacons		Bns in line 270°		270 deg	Leading beacons
121		Beacons marking a clearing line		Bns in line 270°		270 deg	Beacons marking a clearing line or transit
122	Measured Distance 1852 m 090°–270°	Beacons marking measured distance with quoted bearings	MARKERS MARKERS COURSE 270°00' TRUE			270 deg 270 deg	Beacons marking measured distance
123	Y	Cable landing beacon (example)	W				Cable landing beacon (example)

Buoys, Beacons   Q

IALA Maritime Buoyage System

IALA International Association of Marine Aids to Navigation and Lighthouse Authorities

130

Where in force, the IALA System applies to all fixed and floating marks except landfall lights, leading lights and marks, sectored lights and major floating lights. The standard buoy shapes are: cylindrical (can), conical, spherical, pillar, and spar, but variations may occur, for example: minor light floats.

There are two international buoyage regions where lateral marks differ. Each region is primarily comprised of the waters surrounding the areas shown below.

- **Region A**: Greenland, Africa, Europe, Australia and Asia (except for Japan, the Republic of Korea, Taiwan and the Philippines).
- **Region B**: North and South America, Japan, the Republic of Korea, Taiwan and the Philippines.

ECDIS marks the boundary between IALA regions A and B with this symbol: — A — — B — — A — — B — — A — — B — — A — — B — — A — — B —

130.1

Q   Buoys, Beacons

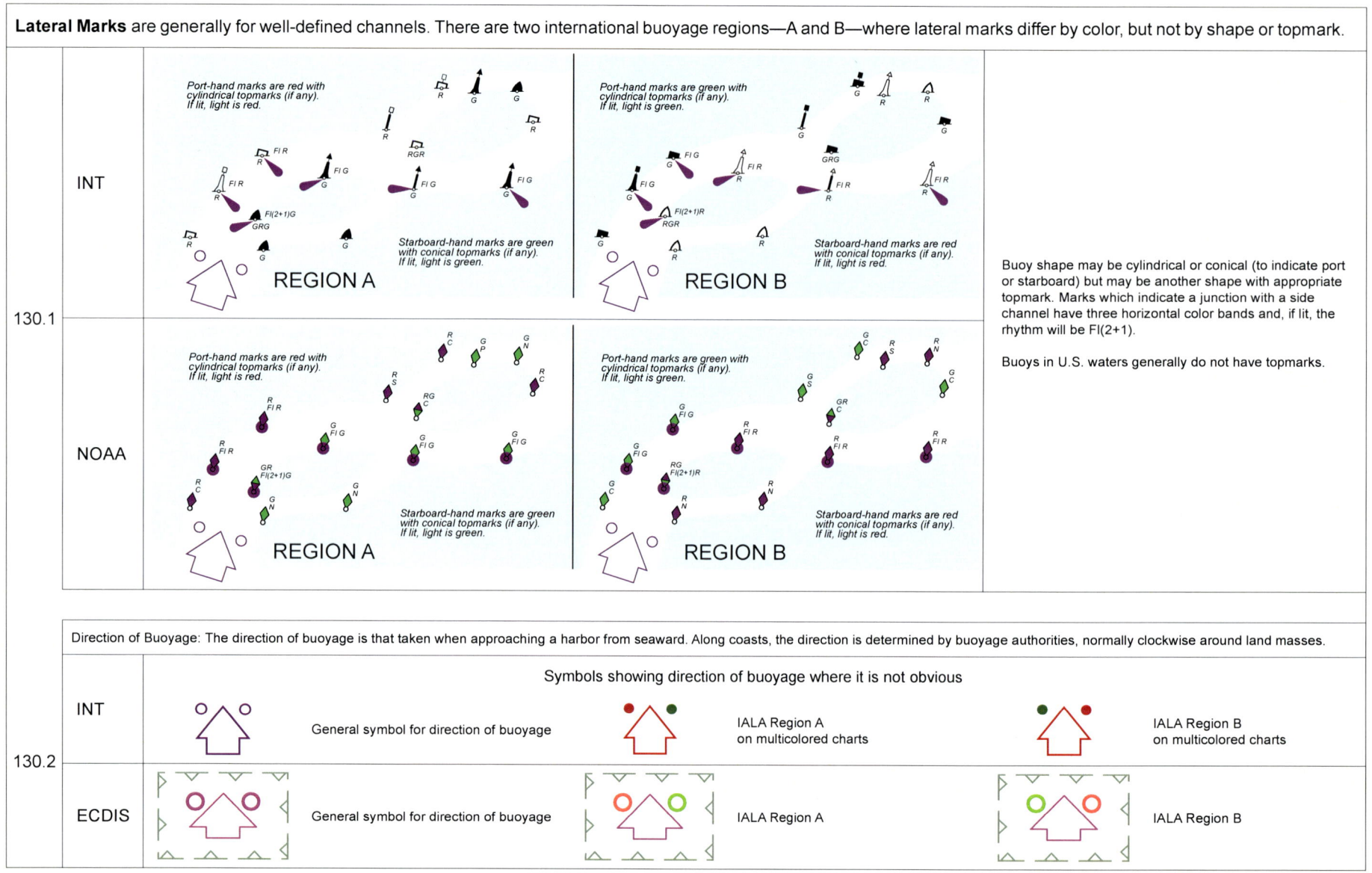

Buoys, Beacons Q

No.	INT	ECDIS
130.3	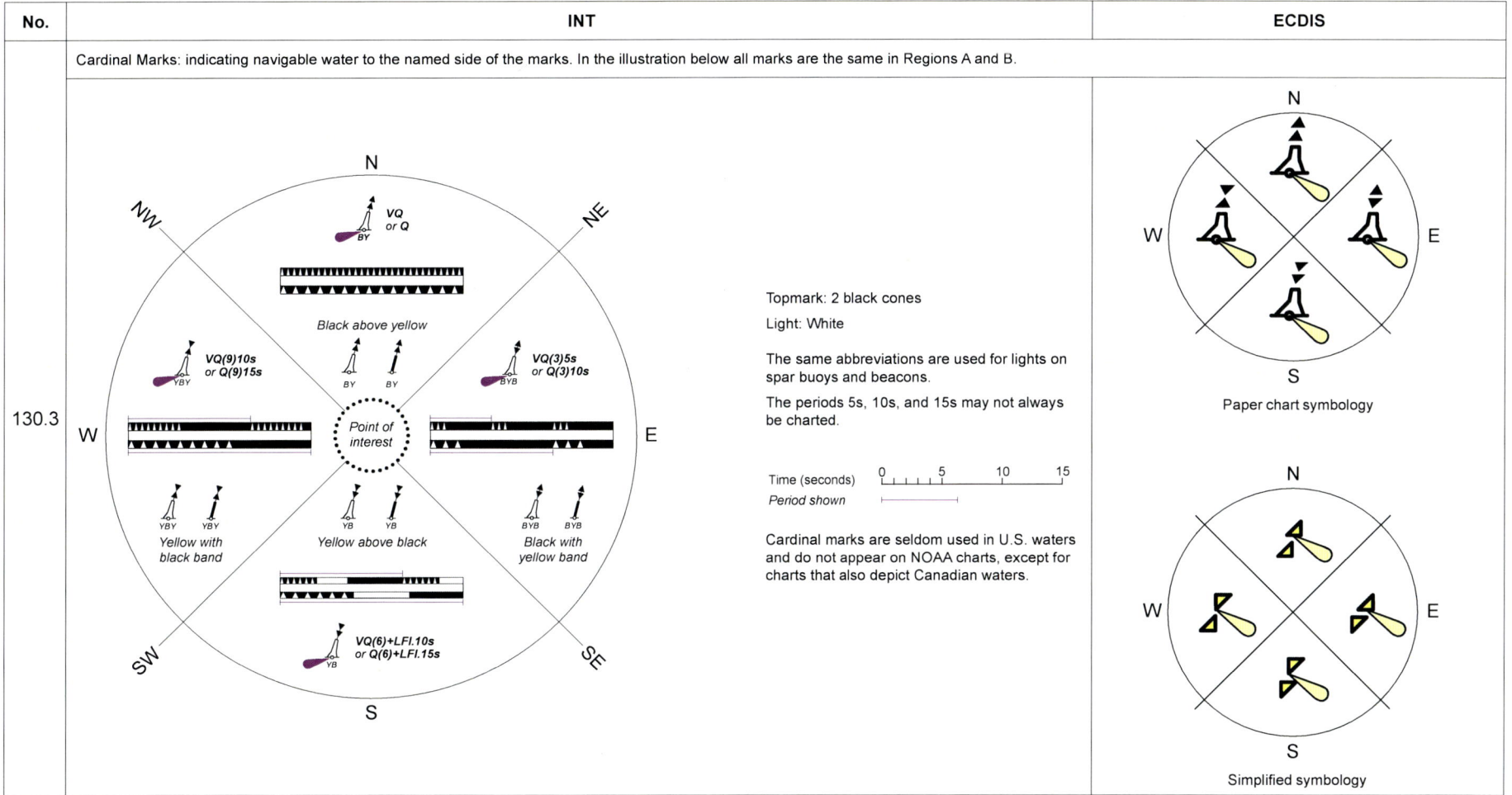 Cardinal Marks: indicating navigable water to the named side of the marks. In the illustration below all marks are the same in Regions A and B. Topmark: 2 black cones Light: White The same abbreviations are used for lights on spar buoys and beacons. The periods 5s, 10s, and 15s may not always be charted. Cardinal marks are seldom used in U.S. waters and do not appear on NOAA charts, except for charts that also depict Canadian waters.	Paper chart symbology Simplified symbology

Q   Buoys, Beacons

No.	INT		Description	NOAA	NGA	Other NGA	ECDIS	
124	🏛 Ref	⬇ Ref	Refuge beacon				✹	Purpose as refuge or firing danger area beacon is obtained by cursor pick
126		⏏	Notice board				⏏	Notice board
130.4	**Isolated Danger Marks** stationed over dangers with navigable water around them. Body: black with red horizontal band(s) Topmark: two black spheres Light: white							
	BRB / BRB		Unlit Marks					Pillar buoy with 2 spheres topmark
	BRB / BRB Fl(2)		Lighted Marks on standard charts	BR				Spar buoy with 2 spheres topmark
	BRB / BRB Fl(2)		Unlit Marks on multicolored charts					Isolated danger buoy, simplified
130.5	**Safe Water Marks**, including mid-channel and landfall marks. Body: red and white vertical stripes Topmark (if any): red sphere Light: white							
	RW / RW / RW		Unlit marks					Spherical buoy, paper chart
	RW / RW / RW Iso or Oc or LFl.10s or Mo(A)		Lighted Marks on standard charts	RW				Pillar buoy with sphere topmark
	RW / RW / RW Iso or Oc or LFl.10s or Mo(A)		Lighted Marks on multicolored charts					Spar buoy with sphere topmark
								Safe water buoy, simplified
130.6	**Special Marks** not primarily to assist navigation but to indicate special features. Body (shape optional): yellow* Topmark (if any): yellow X or upright cross Light: yellow, rhythm optional*							
	Y / Y / Y		Unlit Marks					Spherical buoy, paper chart
	Y / Y / Y Fl Y		Lighted Marks on standard charts	Y				Can buoy
	Y / Y / Y Fl Y		Lighted Marks on multicolored charts					Conical buoy
								Spar buoy with x-shape topmark
								Special purpose buoy, simplified

* In special cases, yellow may be used in conjunction with another color

Buoys, Beacons   Q

No.	INT	Description	NOAA	NGA	Other NGA	ECDIS
130.7	**New Danger Marks**. Body (shape optional): yellow and blue Topmark: yellow cross					
	(unlit marks symbols BuY)	Unlit marks			(pillar and spar buoy symbols)	Pillar buoy with upright cross topmark
	(lighted marks symbols BuY)	Lighted Marks on standard charts				
	(lighted marks yellow BuY)	Lighted Marks on multicolored charts				Spar buoy with upright cross topmark
Supplementary National Symbols						
a		Bell buoy	⚑ BELL	⚑ BELL		
b		Gong buoy	⚑ GONG	⚑ GONG		
c		Whistle buoy	⚑ WHIS	⚑ WHIS		
d		Fairway buoy (red and white vertical stripe)	⚑ RW			
e		Mid-channel buoy (red and white vertical stripe)	⚑ RW			
f		Starboard-hand buoy (entering from seaward - US waters)	⚑ R "2"			
g		Port-hand buoy (entering from seaward - US waters)	⚑ G "1"	⚑ "1"		
h		Bifurcation/Junction buoys	⚑ RG ⚑ GR			
		Isolated danger, Wreck or Obstruction buoy	⚑ BR			
i		Fish trap (area) buoy	⚑ Y			
j		Anchorage buoy (marks limits)	⚑ Y			
l		Triangular shaped beacons	▲ R	△ RG Bn		
		Square shaped beacons	■ G □ GR Bn □ W Bn □ B Bn			
		Beacon, color unknown	□ Bn			
o		Lighted beacon	!	!	! Bn !	
q		Security barrier	– ⚑ Security barrier ⚑ –			
r		Scientific mooring buoy	⚑			
s		Float (unlighted)	⚑			
t		White and blue buoy		△ WBuW		

R   Fog Signals

No.	INT	Description	NOAA	NGA	Other NGA	ECDIS	
General							
Fog Detector Light → P Fog Light → P							
1	AIS	Position of fog signal, type of fog signal not stated	Fog Sig				Position of a conspicuous point feature with fog signal
							Lighted pillar buoy, paper chart with fog signal
							Lighted super-buoy, paper chart with fog signal
2	(man)	Manually activated					
Types of Fog Signals, with Abbreviations						Supplementary national symbol: a	
10	Explos	Explosive	GUN				
11	Dia	Diaphone	DIA				Type of fog signal and its characteristics are obtained by cursor pick
12	Siren	Siren	SIREN				
13	Horn	Horn (nautophone, reed, tyfon)	HORN				
14	Bell	Bell	BELL				
15	Whis	Whistle	WHISTLE				
16	Gong	Gong	GONG				
Examples of Fog Signal Descriptions							
Note: The fog signal symbol will usually be omitted when a description of the signal is given.							
20	Fl.3s 70m 29M Siren Mo(N) 60s	Siren at a lighthouse, giving a long blast followed by a short one (N), repeated every 60 seconds	Fl 3s 70m 29M SIREN Mo(N) 60s	Fl 3s 70m 29M SIREN			Light with fog signal
21	Bell	Wave-actuated bell buoy	BELL	BELL			Pillar buoy, paper chart with fog signal
22	Q(6)+LFl.15s YB Horn(1)15sWhis	Light buoy, with horn giving a single blast every 15 seconds, in conjunction with a wave-actuated whistle	Q(6)+LFl 15s HORN(1) 15s WHIS	Q(6)+LFl 15s YB HORN WHIS		Paper Chart	Simplified	Lighted pillar buoy, paper chart with fog signal
Supplementary National Symbol							
a		Morse Code fog signal	Mo				

Radar, Radio, Satellite Navigation Systems   S

No.	INT	Description	NOAA	NGA	Other NGA	ECDIS	
Radar							
Radar Structures Forming Landmarks → E Radar Surveillance Systems → M							
1	⊙ Ra	Coast radar station, providing range and bearing service on request	⊙ Ra			○	Radio station
2	⊙ Ramark	Ramark, radar beacon transmitting continuously	⊙ Ramark				
3.1	† ⊙ Racon(Z)(3cm)	Radar transponder beacon, with morse identification, responding within the 3 cm (X) band	† ⊙ RACON				
3.2	† ⊙ Racon(Z)(10cm)	Radar transponder beacon, with morse identification, responding within the 10 cm (S) band					
3.3	⊙ Racon(Z)	Radar transponder beacon, with morse identification			⊙ Racon(Z) (3 & 10 cm)		
3.4	⊙ Racon(Z) (Racon Obscd)	Radar transponder beacon with sector of obscured reception				◌ (dashed circle)	Radar transponder beacon
3.4	Racon(Z) ⊙ (Racon(Z) sector)	Radar transponder beacon with sector of reception					
3.5	⊙ ⊙ Racons ⫽ 270° Racon Racon	Leading radar transponder beacons (⫽: objects in line)					
3.5	☆—☆ Lts ⫽ 270° / Racons ⫽ 270° Racon Racon	Leading radar transponder beacons coincident with leading lights					
3.6	⚓ Racon 🛶 Racon	Radar transponder beacons on floating marks	RACON (–) R "2" Fl R 4s	Racon		Paper Chart / Simplified	Radar transponder on floating mark
4	⨳	Radar reflector		⨳ ❗		☀	Symbol indicating this object is radar conspicuous
Radar reflectors are not charted on buoys in regions where they are fitted to nearly all buoys							
5	⨳	Radar conspicuous feature					

S Radar, Radio, Satellite Navigation Systems

No.	INT	Description	NOAA	NGA	Other NGA	ECDIS	
Radio							
Radio Structures Forming Landmarks → E　　Radio Reporting (Calling-in or Way) points → M							
10 †	Name RC	Circular (non-directional) marine or aeromarine radiobeacon	† RC	† R Bn		○	Radio station
11 †	RD 269.5° RD	Directional radiobeacon with bearing line	† RD 270° RD				
†	Lts ≠ 270° RD 270° RD	Directional radiobeacon coincident with leading lights					Additional information regarding radio, such as category of radio station, signal frequency, communication channel, call sign, estimated signal range, periodicity and status may be included in the cursor pick.
12 †	RW	Rotating pattern radiobeacon	†	RW			
13 †	Consol	Consol beacon	† CONSOL Bn 190 kHz MMF	† CONSOL			
14 †	RG	Radio direction-finding station		RDF			The presence of an AIS transmitted signal intended for use as an aid to navigation associated with a physical aid, including the AIS MMSI Number, can be obtained by cursor pick on the physical aid.
15 †	R	Coast radio station providing QTG service	† ○ R Sta	† R			
16 †	Aero RC	Aeronautical radiobeacon	†	AERO R Bn			
17.1	AIS	Automatic Identification System transmitter					
17.2	AIS　　AIS	Automatic Identification System transmitter on floating marks (examples)					
18.1	V-AIS	Virtual AIS (with unknown IALA-defined function)					
18.2	V-AIS　V-AIS　V-AIS　V-AIS	Virtual AIS (with known IALA-defined function)				⬆ V-AIS	North cardinal virtual aid
						⬦ V-AIS	East cardinal virtual aid
						⬇ V-AIS	South cardinal virtual aid
						⊗ V-AIS	West cardinal virtual aid

Radar, Radio, Satellite Navigation Systems   S

No.	INT		Description	NOAA	NGA	Other NGA	ECDIS	
18.3	V-AIS	V-AIS	Virtual AIS with lateral mark function				V-AIS	Port Lateral (IALA B) virtual aid
							V-AIS	Starboard Lateral (IALA B) virtual aid
18.4	V-AIS		Virtual AIS with isolated danger mark function				V-AIS	Isolated Danger virtual aid
18.5	V-AIS		Virtual AIS with safe water mark function				V-AIS	Safe Water virtual aid
18.6	V-AIS		Virtual AIS with special purpose mark function				V-AIS	Special Purpose virtual aid
18.7	V-AIS		Virtual AIS with new danger mark function				V-AIS	Emergency Wreck virtual aid

Satellite Navigation Systems

No.	INT	Description	NOAA	NGA	Other NGA	ECDIS	
50	WGS WGS72 WGS84	World Geodetic System, 1972 or 1984					
	Note: A note may be shown to indicate the shifts of latitude and longitude, to one, two or three decimal places of a minute, depending on the chart scale, which should be made to satellite-derived positions (which are referred to WGS 84) to relate them to the chart.						
51	DGPS	Station providing DGPS corrections				DGPS	DGPS reference station

T Services

No.	INT	Description	NOAA	NGA	Other NGA	ECDIS	
Pilotage							
1.1	◊	Boarding place, position of a pilot cruising vessel	◊ Pilots			◊	Pilot boarding place
1.2	◊ Name	Boarding place, position of a pilot cruising vessel, with name (e.g. District, Port)		◊ Name			
1.3	◊ Note	Boarding place, position of a pilot cruising vessel, with note (e.g. Tanker, Disembarkation)		◊ (see note)		◊ (in dashed ellipse)	Pilot boarding area
1.4	◊ H	Pilots transferred by helicopter					
2	† ■ Pilot Lookout	Pilot office with pilot lookout, Pilot lookout station					
3	■ Pilots	Pilot office	⊙ PIL STA	■ Pilots			
4	Port name (Pilots)	Port with pilotage service (boarding place not shown)					
Coast Guard, Rescue							
10	■ CG ⊙ CG ⌐ CG	Coast Guard station	✦ CG / ⊙ R TR CG WALLIS SANDS			CG	Coast guard station
11	■ CG✦ ⊙ CG✦ ⌐ CG✦	Coast Guard station with Rescue station				CG / ✦	Coast guard station / Rescue station
12	✦	Rescue station, Lifeboat station, Rocket station	✦ LS S				
13	🛥✦ ✦	Lifeboat lying at a mooring				✦	Rescue station
14	Ref Ref	Refuge for shipwrecked mariners					
Signal Stations							
20	⊙ SS	Signal station in general	⊙ SS		⌖ Sig Sta		
21	⊙ SS (INT)	Signal station, showing international port traffic signals				SS	Signal station
22	⊙ SS (Traffic)	Traffic signal station, Port entry and departure signals					
23	⊙ SS (Port Control)	Port control signal station	○ HECP				

Services T

No.	INT	Description	NOAA	NGA	Other NGA	ECDIS	
24	⊙ SS (Lock)	Lock signal station					
25.1	⊙ SS (Bridge)	Bridge passage signal station					
25.2 †	F ★ Traffic-Sig	Bridge lights including traffic signals					
28	⊙ SS (Storm)	Storm signal station		S Sig Sta			
29	⊙ SS (Weather)	Weather signal station, Wind signal station, National Weather Service (NWS) signal station	⊙ NWS SIG STA				
30	⊙ SS (Ice)	Ice signal station				[SS]	Signal station
31	⊙ SS (Time)	Time signal station					
32.1	‡	Tide scale or gauge		○ Tide Gauge			
32.2	⊙ Tide Gauge	Automatically recording tide gauge					
33	⊙ SS (Tide)	Tide signal station					
34	⊙ SS (Stream)	Tidal stream signal station					
35	⊙ SS (Danger)	Danger signal station					
36	⊙ SS (Firing)	Firing practice signal station					
Supplementary National Symbols							
a		Bell (on land)	○ BELL				
b		Marine police station	○ MARINE POLICE				
c		Fireboat station	○ FIREBOAT STATION				
d		Notice board	⚑				
e		Lookout station; Watch tower	⊙ LOOK TR				
f		Semaphore	Sem				
g		Park Ranger station	◉				

U Small Craft (Leisure) Facilities

No.	INT	Description	NOAA	NGA	Other NGA	ECDIS
		Small Craft (Leisure) Facilities				
		Traffic Features, Bridges → D Public Buildings, Cranes → F Pilots, Coast Guard, Rescue, Signal Stations → T				
a		Marina facilities				

			TIDES	DEPTH	SERVICES							BOAT RENTAL						SUPPLIES						
	NO	LOCATION		APPROACH-FEET (REPORTED)	ALONGSIDE-FEET (REPORTED)	ELECTRICITY-MOORINGS-BERTHS (TRANSIENTS)	RAMP SURFACED-NATURAL	REPAIRS HULL-MOTOR-RADIO	MARINE RAILWAY-FEET	LIFT CAPACITY-TONS	CANOE-ROW-MOTOR	CHARTER-HOUSE-SAIL	FOOD-LODGING-CAMPING	TOILETS-SHOWERS-LAUNDRY	PUMP-OUT STATION	WINTER STORAGE WET-DRY	NAUTICAL CHART SALES	WATER-ICE	GROCERIES-HARDWARE	BAIT-TACKLE	DIESEL OIL-GASOLINE
	1	LAS VEGAS BOAT			80	20		S		HM			M		F C	T P	WD	C	WI	GH	BT	G
	2	LAKE MEAD MAR			80	15	B E	S		HM			M		FL	T P	WD	C	WI			DG
	3	HEMENWAY HARBOR			80			S														
	4	TEMPLE BAR HAR			80	15		SN					M	H	FLC	TSL P	WD	C	WI	GH	BT	G
	5	ECHO BAY RESORT			35	35	BM	S	M				M	H	FLC	TSL P	WD	C	WI	GH	BT	G
	6	OVERTON BEACH			100			S					M		F C	TSL	WD		WI	G	BT	G
	7	CALLVILLE BAY M			100	40		S					M	H	F C	TS P	WD		WI	G	B	G

† (+) DENOTES HOURS LATER (-) DENOTES HOURS EARLIER
THE LOCATIONS OF THE ABOVE PUBLIC MARINE FACILITIES ARE SHOWN ON THE CHART BY LARGE PURPLE NUMBERS.
THE TABULATED "APPROACH-FEET (REPORTED)" IS THE DEPTH AVAILABLE FROM THE NEAREST NATURAL OR DREDGED CHANNEL TO THE FACILITY.
THE TABULATED "PUMPING STATION" IS DEFINED AS FACILITIES AVAILABLE FOR PUMPING OUT BOAT HOLDING TANKS.
(H) APPROACH DEPTH FLUCTUATES WITH LAKE LEVELS.

Index of Abbreviations

Note—INT abbreviations are in bold type

A

abt	About	D i
Accom	**Accommodation vessel**	**L 17**
AERO, **Aero**	**Aeronautical light**	P 60–61.1
Aero R Bn	Aeronautical radiobeacon	S 16
Aero RC	**Aeronautical radiobeacon**	S 16
AIS	**Automatic Identification System**	**S 17.1–17.2**
Al	**Alternating**	P 10.11
ALC	**Articulated Load Column**	**L 12**
Am	**Amber**	P 11.8
anc	Ancient	
ANCH, Anch	Anchorage	N 20
ANT, Ant	Antenna	E 31
approx	Approximate	
Apprs	Approaches	
Apr	April	
Apt	Apartment	E s
Arch	Archipelago	
ASL	**Archipelagic Sea Lane**	**M 17**
ATBA	Area To Be Avoided	M 29.1
Aug	August	
auth	Authorized	K 46.2
Ave	Avenue	

B

B	Bay, bayou	
B	**Black**	Q 2
Bdy Mon	Boundary mark (monument)	B 24
Bk	Bank	
bk	Black	J as
bk	**Broken**	J 33
Bkw	Breakwater	F 4.1
bl	Black	J as
BM	Bench Mark	B 23
Bn, Bns	**Beacon(s)**	M 2, P 4–5, Q 80–81
BnTr, BnTrs	Beacon tower(s)	P 3, Q 110
Bo	**Boulder(s)**	J 9.2
Bol	Bollard	
Br	**Breakers**	K 17
br	Brown	J az
brg	Bearing	B 62
brk	Broken	J 33
Bu	**Blue**	P 11.4

C

C	Can, cylindrical	Q 21
C	Cape	
C	Cove	
c	**Coarse**	J 32
Ca, **ca**	**Calcareous**	J 38
CALM	**Catenary Anchor Leg Mooring**	**L 16**
Cap	Capitol	E t
Cas	Castle	E 34.2
Cb	**Cobbles**	J 8
cbl	Cable	B 46
cd	**Candela**	B 54
Cem	Cemetery	E 19
CG	**Coast Guard station**	**T 10**
Ch	Chocolate	J ba
Ch	**Church**	E 10.1
Chan	Channel	
Chem	Chemical	L 40.1–40.2
CHY, **Chy**, **Chys**	**Chimney(s)**	E 22
Cir	Cirripedia	J ae
Ck	Chalk	J f
CL	Clearance	D 20–21, 26, 28
Cl	Clay	J 3
cm	**Centimeter(s)**	B 43
Cn	Cinders	J p
Co	Company	E u
Co	**Coralline Algae**	J 10, K 16
Co Hd	Coral Head	J i
Co rf	Coral reef	
COLREGS	International Regulations for Preventing Collisions at Sea	N a
Consol	**Consol Beacon**	S 13
constr	Construction	F 32
Corp	Corporation	E v
cov	Covers	L 21.2
cps	Cycles per second	B j
Cr	Creek	
CRD	Columbia River Datum	H j
crs	Coarse	J 32
c/s	Cycles per second	B j
Cswy	Causeway	F 3
Ct Ho	Courthouse	E o
Cup	Cupola	E 10.4
Cus Ho	Customs house	F 61
Cy	**Clay**	J 3

D

D	Destroyed	
dec	Decayed	J an
Dec	December	
Deg	Degree(s)	B n
Destr	Destroyed	
dev	Deviation	B 67
DF	Direction Finder	
DG	**Degaussing Range**	N 25, Q 54
DGPS	**Differential Global Positioning System**	S 51
Di	Diatoms	J aa
DIA, **Dia**	**Diaphone**	R 11
Dir	**Direction light**	P 30–31
Discol	Discolored	K e
dist	Distant	
dk	Dark	J bd
dm	Decimeter(s)	B 42
Dn, Dns	**Dolphin(s)**	F 20
Dol	Dolphin(s)	F 20
DW	**Deep Water Route**	M 27.1, N 12.4
DZ	**Danger Zone**	Q 50

E

E	**East**	B 10
ED	**Existence Doubtful**	I 1
EEZ	Exclusive Economic Zone	N 47

Index of Abbreviations

Note—INT abbreviations are in bold type

Entr	Entrance	
ESSA	Environmentally Sensitive Sea Area	N 22
Est	Estuary	
exper	Experimental	
Explos	**Explosive**	**R 10**
Exting, **exting**	**Extinguished**	**P 55**
F		
f	**Fine**	**J 30**
F Fl	**Fixed and flashing**	**P 10.10**
F Gp Fl	**Fixed and Group Flashing**	**P d**
Facty	Factory	E d
FAD	**Fish Aggregating Device**	
Fd	Fjord	
FISH	Fishing	N 21
Fl	**Flashing**	**P 10.4**
fl	Flood	H q
Fla	**Flare stack**	**L 11**
fly	Flinty	J ao
fm, fms	**Fathom(s)**	**B 48**
fne	Fine	J 30
Fog Det Lt	**Fog detector light**	**P 62**
Fog Sig	Fog Signal	R 1
FP	Flagpole	E 27
FPSO	**Floating Production, Storage and Offloading Vessel**	**L 17**
Fr	Foraminifera	J y
Fs, **FS**	**Flagstaff**	**E 27**
Fsh stks	Fishing stakes	K 44.1
FT, **ft**	**Foot, Feet**	**B 47, D 20**
Fu	Fucus	J af
G		
G	**Gravel**	**J 6**
G	**Green**	**P 11.3, Q 2**
G	Gulf	
GAB, Gab	Gable	E i
GCLWD	Gulf Coast Low Water Datum	H k
Gl	Globigerina	J z

glac	Glacial	J ap
gn	Green	J av
Govt Ho	Government House	E m
Gp Fl	Group flashing	P 10.4
Gp Oc	Group occulting	P 10.2
GPS	**Global Positioning System**	
Grd	Ground	J a
Grs	Grass	J v
grt	**Gross Register Tonnage**	
GT	**Gross Tonnage**	
gty	Gritty	J am
gy	Gray	J bb
H		
H	**Helicopter**	**T 1.4**
h	**Hard**	**J 39**
h	**Hour**	**B 49**
HAT	Highest Astronomical Tide	H 3
Hbr Mr	Harbormaster	F 60
HHW	Higher High Water	H b
Hk	Hulk	F 34, K 20–21
Ho	House	
hor	**Horizontally disposed**	**P 15**
Hor CL	Horizontal clearance	D 21
Hosp	Hospital	E g, F 62.2
hr	Hour	B 49
hrd	Hard	J 39
ht	Height	H p
HW	High Water	H a
HWF&C	High Water Full & Change	H h
Hz	Hertz	B g
I		
IALA	International Association of Lighthouse Authorities*	Q 130
IHO	International Hydrographic Organization	
illum	Illuminated	P 63
IMO	International Maritime Organization	

In	Inlet	
in, ins	Inch(es)	B c
Inst	Institute	E n
INT	**International**	**A 2, T 21**
Intens	Intensified	P 46
IQ	Interrupted quick	P 10.6
ISLW	Indian Spring Low Water	H g
Iso	**Isophase**	**P 10.3**
ITZ	Inshore Traffic Zone	M 25.1
IUQ	**Interrupted ultra quick**	**P 10.8**
IVQ	**Interrupted very quick**	**P 10.7**
J		
Jan	January	
Jul	July	
Jun	June	
K		
K	Kelp	J u
kc	Kilocycle	B k
kHz	Kilohertz	B h
km	**Kilometer(s)**	**B 40**
kn	**Knot(s)**	**B 52**
L		
L	Lake, loch, lough	
L Fl	**Long-flashing**	**P 10.5**
La	Lava	J l
Lag	Lagoon	
LANBY	**Large Automatic Navigational Buoy**	**P 6**
LASH	**Lighter Aboard Ship**	
LAT	**Lowest Astronomical Tide**	**H 2**
Lat	**Latitude**	**B 1**
Ldg	**Landing**	**F 17**
Ldg	**Leading Lights**	**P 20.3**
Le	Ledge	
LLW	Lower Low Water	H e
Lndg	**Landing for boats**	**F 17**
LNG	**Liquified Natural Gas**	

*Now known as the International Association of Marine Aids to Navigation and Lighthouse Authorities. The organization, formerly called the International Association of Lighthouse Authorities/Association Internationale de Signalisation Maritime (IALA/AISM), continues to use IALA as an abbreviation for its full name.

Index of Abbreviations
Note—INT abbreviations are in bold type

LoLo	Load-on, Load-off	
Long	Longitude	B 2
LPG	Liquified Petroleum Gas	
Lrg	Large	J a
LS S	Life saving station	T 12
lt	Light	J bc
Lt Ho	Light house	P 1
Lt, Lt(s)	**Light(s)**	P 1
Ltd	Limited	E r
LW	Low Water	H c
LWD	Low Water Datum	H d
LWF&C	Low Water Full and Change	H i
M		
M	**Mud, muddy**	J 2
M	**Nautical mile(s)**	B 45
m	**Medium (in relation to sand)**	J 31
m	**Meter(s)**	B 41
m	**Minute(s) of time**	B 50
Ma	Mattes	J ag
mag	Magnetic	B 61
Magz	Magazine	E l
Maintd	Maintained	P 65
man	**Manually activated**	P 56, R 2
Mar	March	
Mc	Megacycles	B l
Mds	Madrepores	J j
MHHW	Mean Higher High Water	H 13
MHLW	Mean Higher Low Water	H 14
MHW	Mean High Water	H 5
MHWN	Mean High Water Neaps	H 11
MHWS	Mean High Water Springs	H 9
Mi	Nautical mile(s)	B 45
min	Minimum	K 46.2
min	**Minute(s) of time**	B 50
Mk	**Mark**	Q 101
Ml	Marl	J c
MLHW	Mean Lower High Water	H 15
MLLW	Mean Lower Low Water	H 12

MLW	Mean Low Water	H 4
MLWN	Mean Low Water Neaps	H 10
MLWS	Mean Low Water Springs	H 8
mm	**Millimeter(s)**	B 44
Mn	Manganese	J q
Mo	**Morse Code**	P 10.9, R 20
MON, **Mon**	**Monument**	E 24
MR	**Marine Reserve**	N 22
MRCC	**Maritime Rescue and Coordination Center**	
Ms	Mussels	J s
MSL	Mean Sea Level	H 6
Mt	Mountain, Mount	
Mth	Mouth	
MTL	Mean Tide Level	H 1
N		
N	**North**	B 9
N	Nun	Q 20
NE	**Northeast**	B 13
NGA	National Geospatial-Intelligence Agency	
NM	Nautical miles(s)	B 45
NMi	Nautical mile(s)	B 45
No	Number	N 12.2
NOAA	National Oceanic and Atmospheric Administration	
NOS	National Ocean Service	
Nov	November	
Np	Neap tide	H 17
NT	**Net Tonnage**	
NTM	Notice to Mariners	
NW	**Northwest**	B 15
NWS SIG STA	National Weather Service signal station	T 29
O		
Obs Spot	Observation spot	B 21
OBSC, **Obscd**	**Obscured**	P 43
Obstn	**Obstruction**	K 41
Oc	**Occulting**	P 10.2

Occas	**Occasional**	P 50
Oct	October	
ODAS	**Ocean Data Acquisition System**	Q 58
Or	**Orange**	P 11.7
OVHD	Overhead	D 28
Oys	Oysters	J r
P		
P	**Pebbles**	J 7
P	**Pillar**	Q 23
(P)	Preliminary (NTM)	
PA	**Position approximate**	B 7
Pass	Passage, Pass	
Pav	Pavilion	E p
PD	Position doubtful	B 8
Pk	Peak	
PLT STA	Pilot station	T 3
Pm	Pumice	J m
PO	Post office	F 63
Po	Polyzoa	J ad
pos, posn	Position	
Post Off	Post office	F 63
Priv, **priv**	**Private**	P 65, Q 70
Prod well	**Production well**	L 20
PROHIB	Prohibited	N 2.2
PSSA	**Particularly Sensitive Sea Area**	N 22
Pt	Pteropods	J ac
Pyl	**Pylon**	D 26
Q		
Q	**Quick**	P 10.6
QTG	Service producing DF signals	S 15
Quar	Quarantine	F e
Qz	Quartz	J g
R		
R	Coast radio station providing QTC service	S 15
R	Radio Station	S 15
R	**Red**	P 11.2
R, r	**Rock, Rocky**	J 9.1, K b

113

Index of Abbreviations

Note—INT abbreviations are in bold type

R Bn	Circular radiobeacon	S 10
R Lts	Air obstruction lights	P 61.2
R Mast	Radio mast	E 28
R Sta	Radio Station	S 15
R Tower	Radio tower	E 29
R TR, R Tr	Radio tower	E 29
Ra	**Radar**	**M 31–32, S 1**
Ra	Radar reference line	M 32.1
Ra (conspic)	Radar conspicuous point	S 5
Ra Ref	Radar reflector	S 4
Racon	**Radar transponder beacon**	**S 3**
Radar Sc	Radar scanner	E 30.3
Radar Tr, RADAR TR	Radar tower	E 30.2
Ramark	Radar marker beacon	S 2
RC	**Circular radiobeacon**	**S 10**
RD	**Directional radiobeacon**	**S 11**
Rd	Radiolaria	J ab
Rd	Road, roadstead	
rd	Red	J ay
RDF	Radio direction finding station	S 14
Ref	**Refuge**	**Q 124**
Rep	Reported	I 3
Rf	Reef	
RG	Radio direction finding station	S 14
Rk	Rocks	J 9.1, K b
Rky	Rocky	J 9.1
RoRo	**Roll-on, Roll-off Ferry (RoRo Terminal)**	**F 50**
rt	Rotten	J aj
Ru, (ru)	**Ruin, ruined**	**D 8, E 25.2, F 33**
RW	**Rotating-pattern radiobeacon**	**S 12**
S		
S	Sand	J 1
S	South	B 11
S	Spar, spindle	Q 24
s	**Second(s) of time**	**B 51, P 12**
SALM	**Single Anchor Leg Mooring**	**L 12**
SBM	**Single Buoy Mooring**	**L 16**
Sc	Scanner	E 30.3
Sc	Scoriae	J o
Sch	Schist	J h
Sch	School	E f
SD	Sailing Directions	
Sd	Sound	
SD	Sounding doubtful	I 2
SE	**Southeast**	**B 14**
sec	**Seconds of time**	**B 51**
Sep	September	
sf	**Stiff**	**J 36**
sft	Soft	J 35
Sg	**Seagrass**	**J 13.3**
Sh	**Shells**	**J 11**
Shl	Shoal	
Si	**Silt**	**J 4**
Sig	**Signal**	**R 1, T 25.2**
Sig Sta	Signal station	T 20
S-L Fl	Short-Long Flashing	P b
S/M	Sand over mud	J 12.1
sml	Small	J ah
SMt	Seamount	
Sn	Shingle	J d
so	**Soft**	**J 35**
Sp	Church spire	E 10.3
SP	Spherical	Q 22
Sp	spire	E 10.3
Sp	Spring tide	H 16
Spg	Sponge	J t
Spi	Spicules	J x
Spipe, S'pipe	Standpipe	E 21
spk	Speckled	J al
SPM	**Single Point Mooring**	**L 12**
SS	**Signal station**	**T 20–36**
St	**Stones**	**J 5**
St M, St Mi	Statute mile(s)	B e
STA, Sta	Station	F 41.1, S 15, T 3
stf	Stiff	J 36
Stg	Sea-tangle	J w
stk	Sticky	J 34
Str	Strait	
Str	Stream	H l
str	Streaky	J ak
sub	Submarine	K d
Subm	Submerged	K 43.1
SW	**Southwest**	**B 16**
sy	**Sticky**	**J 34**
T		
T	Short ton(s)	B m
T	Telephone	E q
T	TRUE	B 63
T	Tufa	J n
t	**Ton(s), Tonnage (weight)**	**B 53, F 53**
Tel	Telegraph	D 27
Tel off	Telegraph office	E k
Temp, **temp**	**Temporary**	**P 54**
ten	Tenacious	J aq
Tk	Tank	E 32
TR, **Tr**, **Trs**	**Tower(s)**	**E 10.2, E 20**
TSS	Traffic Separation Scheme	M 20.1
TT	Tree tops	C 14
TV Mast	Television mast	E 28
TV Tower	Television tower	E 29
U		
ULCC	**Ultra Large Crude Carrier**	
Uncov	Uncovers	K 11
unev	Uneven	J bf
Univ	University	E h
UQ	**Ultra quick**	**P 10.8**
UTC	Coordinated Universal Time	
UTM	Universal Transverse Mercator	
V		
v	Volcanic	J 37

Index of Abbreviations

Note—INT abbreviations are in bold type

var, VAR	Variation	B 60
vard	Varied	J be
vel	Velocity	H n
vert	**Vertically disposed**	P 15
Vert CL	Vertical clearance	D 20, 28
Vi	**Violet**	P 11.5
Vil	Village	D 4
VLCC	**Very Large Crude Carrier**	G 187
vol	Volcanic, Volcano	J 37
Vol Ash	Volcanic ash	J k
VQ	**Very quick**	P 10.7
VTS	**Vessel Traffic Service**	
W		
W	**West**	B 12
W	**White**	P 11.1
Wd	**Weed**	J 13.1
Well	**Wellhead**	L 21
WGS	**World Geodetic System**	S 50
Wh	White	J ar
Whf	Wharf	F 13
WHIS, **Whis**	**Whistle**	R 15
Wk, Wks	**Wreck(s)**	K 20
Wtr Tr, WTR TR	Water tower	E 21
Y		
Y	**Yellow, Orange, Amber**	P 11.6–11.8
yd, yds	Yard(s)	B d
yl	Yellow	J aw
μ		
μs, μsec	Microsecond(s)	B f

Index

A

Abandoned railroad	D c
Accommodation vessel	L 17
Accurate position	B 32, E 2
Aerial	
cableway	D 25
dish	E 31
Aero light	P 60
Aeronautical radiobeacon	S 16
Air obstruction light	P 61.1–61.2
Airfield	D 17
Airport	D 17
AIS	S 17.1–17.2
All-round light	P 42.1–43.2
Alternate course	M c
Alternating light	P 10.11
Amber	P 11.8
Anchor berth	N 11.1–11.2
Anchorage	
areas	N 10–14
buoy	Q j
for sea-planes	N 14
Anchoring prohibited	N 20
Annual change	B 70
Anomaly, magnetic	B 82.1–82.2
Antenna	E 31
Apparent shoreline	C p
Approximate	
depth contour	I 31
height of top of trees	C 14
position	B 7, 33, E 2
topographic contour	C 12
vertical clearance	D i
Aquaculture	K 44.1–48.2
Archipelagic Sea Lane (ASL)	M 17
Areas	N
pipeline	L 40.2, L 41.2
restricted	M 14, N 2.1
to be avoided	M 14, 29.1–29.2
wire drag	I 24
Articulated Loading Column (ALC)	L 12
Ash, volcanic	J k
Astronomical tide	H 2–3

Automatic Identification System (AIS) transmitter	S 17.1–17.2
Awash, rock	K 12

B

Band, S & X	S 3.1–3.2
Bar code	A d
Barrage, flood	F 43
Barrel buoy	Q 25
Barrier	
floating	F 29.1
oil retention	F 29.2
security	F 29.1, Q q
Bascule bridge	D 23.4
Basin	F 27–28
Battery	E 34.3
Battery (fortification)	E 34.3
Beacon	Q 80–126
articulated	P 5
buoyant	P 5
leading	Q 102.2, 120
lighted	P 3–5
marking a clearing line	Q 121
marking measured distance	Q 122
on submerged rock	Q 83
radar	S 2–3.6
radio	S 10–16
resilient	P 5
topmarks	Q 9–11, 82, 102.1
towers	P 3, Q 110–111
Bearing	B r
Being reclaimed	F 31
Bell	R 14
buoy	Q a, R 21
on land	T a
Benchmark	B o
Berth	
anchor	N 11.1–11.2
dangerous cargo	F 19.3
designation	F 19.1, N 11.1–11.2, Q 42
visitors	F 19.2
yacht	F 11.2
Bifurcation buoy	Q h
Black	J as, Q 2
Blind, duck	K j–k
Blockhouse	E 34.2
Blue	J au, P 11.4

Board (leading beacon)	Q 102.2
Boarding place, pilot	T 1.1–1.4
Boat harbor, marina	F 11.1
Boom	F 29.1
Boulders	J 9.2
international	N 40–41
Boundary	
IALA region	Q 130
Breakers	C d, K 17
Breakwater	F 4.1–4.3
Bridge	D 20.1–24
bascule	D 23.4
draw	D 23.6
fixed	D 20.1
lifting	D 23.3
light (traffic signal)	T 25.2
passage signal station	T 25.1
pontoon	D 23.5
swing	D 23.2
transporter	D 24
under construction	D d
Broken	J 33
Brown	J az
Bubbler curtain, bubbler	F 29.2
Buildings	D 2, 5–6, 8
Buoyage system, IALA	Q 130–130.7
Buoyant beacon	P 5
Buoy	Q 20–71
cardinal	Q 130.3
isolated danger	Q 130.4
lateral	Q 130.1
mooring	Q 40–45
new danger	Q 130.7
safe water	Q 130.5
scientific mooring	Q r
special	Q 130.6
Buried pipeline	L 42.1
Bushes	C o

C

Cable	
ferry	M 51
landing beacon	Q 123
overhead	D 26–27, H 20
submarine	L 30.1–32
Cableway (aerial)	D 25
Cairn	Q 100

Index

CALM (Catenary Anchor Leg Mooring)	L 16
Caisson	F 42
Calcareous	J 38
Calling-in point	M 40.1
Calvary cross	E 24
Camping site	E 37.1–37.2
Can buoy	Q 21
Canal	F 40
distance mark	B 25.1–25.2
Candela	B 54
Cardinal marks	Q 130.3
Careening grid	F 24
Cargo transhipment area	N 64
Castle	E 34.2
Casuarina	C 31.6
Causeway	F 3
Cautionary notes	A 16
Cemetery	E 19
Centimeter	B 43
Chalk	J f
Channel	I 20–22
Chart	
datum	A 3, C a, H 1, 20
dimension	A 8
number	A 1–2
reference to another	A 18–19
scale	A 13
title	A 10
Chemical dumping ground	N 24
Chemical pipeline	L 40.1–40.2
Chimney	E 22
Chocolate	J ba
Church	E 10.1
dome	E 10.4
spire	E 10.3
tower	E 10.2
Cinders	J p
Circular (non-directional) aeromarine radiobeacon	S 10
Circular (non-directional) marine radiobeacon	S 10
Cirripedia	J ae
Clay	J 3
Clearance	
horizontal	D 21
safe vertical	D 26, i
vertical	D 22, 23.1, 23.4, 23.6–28
Cleared platform	L 22
Clearing line	M 2
Clearing line beacon	Q 121
Cliffs	C 3
Coal head	J i
Coarse	J 32
Coast	
flat	C 5
radar station	S 1
radio station providing QTG service	S 15
steep	C 3
Coast Guard station	T 10–11
Coastline	C 1–8
surveyed	C 1
unsurveyed	C 2
Cobbles	J 8
Colored mark	Q 101
Colored topmark	Q 102.1
Colors	
beacons	Q 2–5
buoys	Q 2–5
lights	P 11.1–11.8
topmarks	Q 2–5
COLREGS demarcation line	N a
Columbia River Datum	H j
Column	E 24
Compass rose	A c, B 70
Composite	
group-flashing	P 10.4
group-occulting	P 10.2
Conical buoy	Q 20
Conifer	C 31.3, j
Consol beacon	S 13
Conspicuous landmark	E 2
Conspicuous, radar	S 5
Container crane	F 53.2
Contiguous zone	N 44
Continental shelf	N 46
Continuous	
quick	P 10.6
ultra quick	P 10.8
very quick	P 10.7
Contour	
depth	I 30–31
drying	I 15, 30
topographic	C 10, 12, H 20
Control point	B 20–24
Conversion scales	A a
Conveyor	F g
Copyright note	A 5
Coral	J 10, 22, K 16, h, m
Coral reef	
always covers	K 16
covers and uncovers	J 22, K m
detached	K h
Coralline algae	J 10
Corner coordinates	A 9
Covers	J 21–22, K 11, 16, 21
Crane	F 53.1–53.3
Crib	K i–j, L 43, b
Crossing gates	M 22
Crossing, traffic separation	M 23
Cubic meter	B b
Cultivated	
fields	C l
shellfish	K 47
Cultural features	D
Cupola	E 10.4
Current	H 42–43, m, t
diagram	H t
in restricted waters	H 42
Customs	
house	F 61
limit	N 48
office	F 61
Cutting	D 14
Cycles per second	B j
Cylindrical buoy	Q 21
Cypress buoy	C r

Index

D

Dam	F 44
Danger	
firing area	N 30, Q 50, 125
isolated mark	Q 130.4
line	K 1
signal station	T 35
zone	Q 50
Dangerous	
cargo berth	F 19.3
rock	K 10–13, 14.2
wreck	K 28
Dark	J bd
Data collection buoy	Q 58
Datum	
chart	H 1, 20
sounding reduction	H 1
Daymark (dayboard)	Q 10, 80–81, 110, l
Daytime light	P 51
Deadhead	K 43.2
Decayed	J an
Deciduous	
woodland	C i
Decimeter	B 42
Deep water	
anchorage area	N 12.4
route	M 27.1–27.3
Degaussing range	N 25
buoy	Q 54
Degree	B 4
Depth	
charted	H 20
contours	I 30
minimum	K 46.2, M 27.2
observed	H 20
out of position	I 11
safe clearance	K 3, 30, f
swept	I 24, a, b, K 2, 27, 42, f
units used for	A b
unknown	K 3, 13, 23, 28, 30, 40, a, L 21.1
Depths	I
Derrick, oil	L 10
Designation of	
beacon	Q 10
berth	F 19.1
buoy	Q 11
platform	L 2
reporting point	M 40.1
tidal stream, position of tabulated data	H 46
transit shed	F 51
Detector light	P 62
Development area	L 4
Deviation	
dolphin	F 21
DGPS correction transmitter	S 51
Diaphone	R 11
Diatoms	J aa
Diffuser	L 43
Dike	F 1
Direction	
of buoyage	Q 130.2
finding, radio station	S 14
of flow	F 44
light	P 30.1–31
of traffic	M 10, 11, 26.1–26.2, 40.1
Directional radiobeacon	S 11
Directions, compass	B
Discolored water	K e
Dish aerial	E 31
Disposition of lights	P 15
Distance	B
along waterway	B 25.1–25.2
measured, beacons marking	Q 122
Disused	
pipeline/pipe	L 44
platform	L 14
submarine cable	L 32
Diurnal tide	H 30
Dock	
dry, graving	F 25
floating	F 26
wet	F 27
Dolphin	F 20–21
Dome	E 30.4
Doubtful	
depth	I 2
existence	I 1
position	B 8
Draft	M 6, N 12.4
area	I 20–22
channel	I 20–22
Dredging (extraction) area	N 63
Drying	
contour	I 30
height	H 20, I 15
Duck blind	K j–k
Dumping ground	N c, d, g
chemical waste	N 24
explosives	N 23.1–23.2
Dunes	C 8

E

East	B 10
cardinal mark	Q 130.3
Ebb tide stream	H 41
Eddies	H 45
Edition note	A 6
Eelgrass	C t
Elevation of light	H 20, P 13
Ellipsoid	A 3
Embankment	D 15
Entry prohibited area	N 2.2, 31
Environmentally Sensitive Sea Area (ESSA)	N 22
Established (mandatory) direction of traffic flow	M 10
Eucalypt	C 31.8
Evergreen	C 31.2
Example of	
conspicuous landmarks	E 2
fog signal descriptions	R 20–22
full light description	P 16
landmarks	E 1
routing measures	M 18–29.2
Exclusive Economic Zone (EEZ)	N 47
Exercise area, submarine	N 33
Existence doubtful	I 1
Explanatory notes	A 11, 16
Explosive fog signal	R 10
Explosives	
anchorage area	N 12.7
dumping ground	N 23.1–23.2
Extinguished light	P 55

Index

Extraction area	N 63

F

Factory	E d
Faint sector	P 45.1–45.2
Fairway	M 18
Farm	
marine	K 48.1–48.2
wave	L 6
wind	L 5.2
Fast ice, limit	N 60.1
Fathom(s)	B 48
Feet	B 47
Fence	D g
Ferry	M 50–51
terminal, RoRo	F 50
Filao	C 31.7
Fine	J 30
Fireboat station	T c
Firing	
danger area	N 30
danger area buoy	Q 50
practice signal station	T 36
Fish	
haven	K 46.1–46.2
marine farm	K 48.1–48.2
trap	K 44.2–45, Q i
weir	K 44.2
Fishery zone limit	N 45
Fishing	
harbor	F 10
limit (fish trap area)	N b
prohibited	N 21.1
stakes	K 44.1
Fixed	
bridge	D 20.1
flashing, and	P 10.10, d
light	P 10.1
point	B 22
Flagstaff, Flagpole	E 27
Flare stack	E 23, L 11
Flashing light	P 10.4
Flat coast	C 5
Flinty	J ao
Float	K q, Q s

Floating	
barrier	F 29.1
dock	F 26
oil barrier	F 29.1
wind farm	L 5.2
wind turbine	L 5.1
Flood	H q
barrage	F 43
tide (stream)	H 40
Floodlit, floodlight	P 63
Fog	
detector light	P 62
light	P 52
signals	R
Foot	B 47
Footbridge	D 20.2
Foraminifera	J y
Foreshore	C c
Form lines	C 13
Fort	E 34.2
Fortified structure	E 34.1
Foul	
area	K o
ground	K 31.1–31.2
Front light	P 23
Fucus	J af

G

Gable	E i
Gas	
pipe line	L 40.1
pipeline area	L 40.2
Gasfield name	L 1
Gate	F 42
Geographical positions	B 1–16
Glacial	J ap
Glacier	C 25
Globigerina	J z
Glossary	A e
Gong	R 16, Q b
Grass	C s, J v
Grassfields	C m
area with	J 20
Gravel	C c, J 6, 20

Graving dock	F 25
Gray	J bb
Green	J av, P 11.3, Q 2
Gridiron	F 24
Gritty	J am
Groin	F 6
Ground	J a
tackle	Q 42
Group	
fixed and flashing	P d
flashing	P 10.4
occulting	P 10.2
quick	P 10.6
short flashing	P c
very quick	P 10.7
Gulf Coast Low Water Datum	H k
Gulf Stream limits	H u
Gun	R 10

H

Hachures	C f
Harbor	
installations	F 10–34
limit	N 49
master's office	F 60
Harbors	F
Hard	J 39
Health office	F 62.1
Height	H p
datum	H 20
drying	H 20, I 15
light (elevation of)	H 20, P 13
rocks	K 10–11
spot	C 10–11, 13, H 20
of structure	E 4–5
tide	H 20, P 13
of top of trees	C 14
of wellhead	L 23
Heliport, Helipad	D 18
Hertz	B g
High water	H 20, a
High Water Full and Change	H h
Higher High Water	H 20, b
Highest Astronomical Tide (HAT)	H 3
Highway	D 10
markers	D a

Index

Hillocks	C 4
Horizontal	
light	P 15
clearance	D 21
Horizontally disposed	P 15
Horn	R 13
Hospital	E g, F 62.2
Hour	B 49
Hulk	F 34, K 20–21, 23

I

IALA Maritime Buoyage System	Q 130
Ice	
boom	F 29.1
fast (ice front)	N 60.1
sea ice (pack ice) seasonal	N 60.2
signal station	T 30
Illuminated	P 63
Imprint	A 4
Inadequately surveyed area	I 25
Inch	B c
Incineration area	N 65
Indian Spring Low Water	H g
Inshore traffic zone	M 25.1–25.2
Installations, offshore	L
Intake pipe	L 41.1–41.2, b
Intense	P 46.1–46.2
Intensified sector	P 46.1–46.2
Intermittent river	C 21
International	
boundary	N 40–41
chart number	A 2
nautical mile, sea mile	B 45
Interrupted light	
quick	P 10.6
ultra quick	P 10.8
very quick	P 10.7
Intertidal area	J 20–22
Isogonic lines (Isogonals)	B 71
Isolated danger mark	Q 130.4
Isophase light	P 10.3

J

Jetty	F 14, a–c
Joss house	E 13

K

Kelp	J 13.1–13.2, u
Kilocycle	B k
Kilohertz	B h
Kilometer	B 40
Knot	B 52, H o

L

Lake	C 21, 23
intermittent	C 21
LANBY	P f
Landing	
beacon (cable)	Q 123
boats, for	F 17
seaplanes, for	N 13
stairs	F 18
Landmarks	E
Lane, submarine transit	N 33
Large	J ai
Large Automatic Navigational Buoy (LANBY)	P f
Lateral marks (IALA System)	Q 130.1
Latitude	B 1
Lattice beacon	Q 111
Lava	C 26, J 9, l
Layout of chart	A
Leading	
beacons	Q 120
lights	P 20.1–23
line	M 1
Least depth	K 26–27, 30
in narrow channel	I 12
Leisure facilities	U
Levee	F 1
Lifeboat	T 12–13
mooring	T 13
station	T 12
Lifting bridge	D 23.3
Light	J bc
arc of visibility, with restricted	P 44.1–44.2
character	P 10.1–11.8
chart limits, off	P 8
color	P 11.1–11.8
description	P 16
direction	P 30.1–31
disposition	P 15
elevation	P 13
exhibited only when specially needed	P 50
faint sector, with	P 45.1–45.2
float	Q 30.1–31
in line	P 21.1–21.2
intensified sector, with	P 46.1–46.2
landmarks, on	P 7
leading	P 20.1–23
marking fairway	P 20.1–23
Moiré effect	P 31
period	P 12
range	P 14
sector	P 40.1–46.2
special	P 60–66
structures	P 1–7
synchronized	P 66
times of exhibition	P 50–55
vessel	P e, Q 32
Light characters	P 10.1–10.11
Lighted	
beacon	P 4, Q o
beacon tower	P 3
marks	Q 7–8
mooring buoy	Q 41
offshore platform	P 2.1–2.2
Lighthouse	P 1
Lights	P
Lights exhibited only when specially needed	P 50
Lights in line	P 21.1–21.2
Lights Marking Fairways	P 20.1–23
Lights with limited times of exhibition	P 50–55
Limit of	
area feature in general	C q
area into which entry is prohibited	N 2.2, 31
contiguous zone	N 44
continental shelf	N 46
danger line	K 1
development area	L 4
dredged area	I 20
Exclusive Economic Zone (EEZ)	N 47
fast ice	N 60.1
fishery zone	N 45
fishing area	N b
Gulf Stream	H u
nature reserve	N 22
no discharge zone	N i
restricted area	M 14, N 2.1
routing measure	M 14–15

Index

safety zone	L 3
sea ice (pack ice) seasonal	N 60.2
unsurveyed area	I 25
Linear scale	A 14–15
Local magnetic anomaly	B 82.1–82.2
Lock	F 41.1–41.2
signal station	T 24
Log pond	F 29.1
Logo	A 12
Long-flashing light	P 10.5
Longitude	B 2
Lookout	
pilot	T 2
station	T e
Low water	H 20, c
line	I 30
Lower light	P 23
Lower low datum	H d
Lower low water	H e
Lower water full & change	H i
Lowest Astronomical Tide (LAT)	H 2

M

Madrepores	J j
Magnetic	B q
anomaly	B 82.1–82.2
compass	B 68.1–71
variation	B 68.1–71, p
Main light visible all-round	P 42.1–42.2
Major	
light	P 1
light off chart limits	P 8
Manganese	J q
Mangrove	C 32
Manually activated	P 56, R 2
Marabout	E 13
Marginal notes	A
Marina	F 11.1
facilities	U a
Marine	
farm	K 48.1–48.2
reserve	N 22
Maritime limit	N 1.1–1.2

Marks	
cardinal	Q 130.3
colored	Q 101
isolated danger	Q 130.4
lateral	Q 130.1
lighted	Q 7–8
minor	Q 90–102.2
new danger	Q 130.7
safe water	Q 130.5
special	Q 130.6
wreck (new danger)	Q 130.7
Marl	J c
Marsh	C 33
Mast	
radar	E 30.1
radio, television	E 28
wreck	K 25
Mattes	J ag
Maximum	
authorized draft	M 6
speed	N 27
Mean	
High Water (MHW)	H 5, 20, 30
High Water Neaps (MHWN)	H 11
High Water Springs (MHWS)	H 9
Higher High Water (MHHW)	H 13, 30
Higher Low Water (MHLW)	H 14
Low Water (MLW)	H 4, 20, 30
Low Water Neaps (MLWN)	H 10
Low Water Springs (MLWS)	H 8
Lower High Water (MLHW)	H 15
Lower Low Water (MLLW)	H 12, 20, 30
Sea Level (MSL)	H 6, 20
tide level	H f
Measured Distance	Q 122
Medium	J 31
Megacycle	B l
Megahertz	B i
Meter	B 41
Microsecond	B f
Mid-channel buoy	Q e
Mile	
nautical (sea mile)	A 15, B 45
statute	B 25.1–25.2, e
three nautical mile line	N h
Military area	N 30–34
Millimeter	B 44
Minaret	E 17
Mine (explosive)	N 23.1

Mine (ore extraction)	E 36
Minefield	N 34
Mine-laying practice area	N 32
Minor	
impermanent marks	Q 90–92
light	P 1, note after P 5
light floats	Q 30.1–31
marks	Q 100–102.2
pile	F 22
post	F 22
Minute	
of arc	B 5
of time	B 50
Mixed bottom	J 12.1–12.2
Moiré effect light	P 31
Mole	F 12
Monument	E 24
Moored storage tanker	L 17
Mooring	
berth number	Q 42
canal	F f
ground tackle	L 18, Q 42
life boat	T 13
numerous	Q 44
scientific mooring buoy	Q r
Single Buoy (SBM)	L 16
Single Point (SPM)	L 12
trot	Q 42
visitors'	Q 45
buoy	Q 40–45
lighted	Q 41
tanker	L 16
telegraphic	Q 43
telephonic	Q 43
Morse Code	
fog signal	R a
light	P 10.9
Mosque	E 17
Motorway	D 10
Mud	C c, J 2
Muslim shrine	E a
Mussels	J s

N

National	
limits	N 40–49
park	N 22
Natural	
features	C
watercourse	I 16

Index

Nature	
reserve	N 22
of the seabed	J
Nautical mile	B 45
Nautophone	R 13
Neap tide	H 10–11, 17, 30–31
Nets, tunny	K 44.2–45
New	
edition date	A 6
danger mark	Q 130.7
Nipa palm	C 31.5, 32
No anchoring area	N 20
No bottom found	I 13
No discharge zone	N i
Non-dangerous wreck	K 15, 29
Non-directional radiobeacon	S 10
Non-tidal basin	F 27
North	B 9
cardinal mark	Q 130.3
Northeast	B 13
Northwest	B 15
Notes	A 11, 16
Notice board	Q 126, T d
Notice to mariners	A 7
Nun buoy	Q 20

O

Obelisk	E 24
Obscured sector	P 43.1–43.2
Observation spot	B 21
Obstruction	K 40–48.2
light, air	P 61.1–61.2
Occasional light	P 50
Occulting light	P 10.2
Ocean current	H 43
ODAS buoy	L 25, Q 58
Office	
customs	F 61
harbormaster's	F 60
health	F 62.1
pilot	T 2–3
quarantine	F e

Offshore	
Installations	L
platform, lighted	P 2.1–2.2
position, tidal levels	H 47
Ogival buoy	Q 20
Oil	
barrier	F 29.1–29.2
derrick	L 10
installation buoy, Catenary Anchor Leg Mooring (CALM)	L 16
pipeline	L 40.1
pipeline area	L 40.2
Oilfield with name	L 1
One-way track	M 5.1–5.2, 27.3
Ooze	J b
Opening bridge	D 23.1
Orange	J ax, P 11.7
Ordnance, unexploded	K p
Outfall pipe	L 41.1–41.2
Overfalls	H 44
Overhead	
cable	D 27
pipe	D 28
transporter	D 25
Oysters	J r

P

Pack ice, limit	N 60.2
Paddy field	C n
Pagoda	E 13
Painted board	Q 102.2
Palm	C 31.4
Park ranger station	T g
Particularly Sensitive Sea Area (PSSA)	N 22
Patent slip	F 23
Path	D 12
Pebbles	J 7
Perch	Q 91
Period of light	P 12
Pictorial sketches	E 3.1–3.2
Pier	F 14
promenade	F 15
ruined	F 33.2

Pile	F 22
submerged	K 43.1–43.2
Pillar	
buoy	Q 23
monument	E 24
Pilot	T 1–4
boarding place	T 1.1–1.3
helicopter transfer	T 1.4
look out	T 2
office	T 2–3
Pilotage	T 1–4
Pipe	
intake	L 41.1–41.2, b
outfall	L 41.1–41.2
overhead	D 28
pneumatic (bubbler)	F 29.2
Pipeline	
buried	L 42.1
land, on	D 29
overhead	D 28
submarine	L 40.1–44
tunnel	L 42.2
Platform	L 2, 10, 13–14, 22, P 2
cleared	L 22
submerged	K l
Point	
base point for territorial sea baseline	N 42
fixed	B 22
Single Point Mooring (SPM)	L 12
symbols, position	B 32–33
triangulation	B 20
Pole	Q 90
Police station, marine	T b
Polyzoa	J ad
Pontoon	F 16
bridge	D 23.5
Port	
pilotage service, with	T 4
signal station	T 21–23
Ports	F
Position	
accurate	B 2, E 2
approximate	B 7, E 2
of buoy or beacon	Q 1
doubtful	B 8
of fog signal	R 1
of pilot cruising vessel	T 1.1–1.3
tidal levels	H 47
tidal stream data	H 46

Index

Positions	B
symbolized	B 30–33
Post	F 22, K 43.1
covers and uncovers	K r
office	F 63
submerged	K 43.1
Power	
overhead cable	D 26, H 20
submarine cable	L 31.1–31.2
transmission line	D h
Practice area (military)	N 30–34
Precautionary area	M 16, M 24
Preferred channel buoy	Q 130.1
Private	
buoy	Q 70
light	P 50, 65
Production	
platform	L 10
well	L 20
Prohibited	
anchoring	N 20
area	N 2.2, 31
diving	N 21.2
fishing	N 21.1
Promenade pier	F 15
Protective structures	F 1–6.3
Pteropods	J ac
Public Buildings	F 60–63
Publication note	A 4
Pumice	J m
Pump-out facilities	F d
Pylon	D 26, E 29
Q	
QTG service	S 15
Qualifying Terms	J 30–39
Quarantine	
anchorage area	N 12.8
building, health office	F 62.1
office	F e
Quarry	E 35.1–35.2
Quartz	J g
Quay	F 13
Quick light	P 10.6

R	
Races	H 44
Racon	S 3.1–3.6
Radar	
beacon	S 2–3.6
conspicuous feature	S 5
dome (radome)	E 30.4
mast	E 30.1
range	M 31
reference line	M 32.1–32.2
reflector	Q 10–11, S 4
scanner	E 30.3
station	S 1
surveillance system	M 30–32.2
tower	E 30.2
transponder beacon, racon	S 3.1–3.6
transponder beacons on floating marks	S 3.6
tower	E 29
Radio	S 10–18.7
direction-finding station	S 14
mast	E 28
repoting line	M 40.2
reporting point, calling-in or way point	M 40.1
station, QTG service	S 15
Radiobeacon	S 10–16
Radiolaria	J ab
Radome	E 30.4
Railway	D 13, b
station	D 13
Ramark	S 2
Ramp	F 23
Range	P 14
Rapids	C 22
Rate	H n
Rear light	P 22
Reclamation area	F 31
Recommended	
deep water track	M 27.3, a–b
direction of traffic flow	M 11, 26.1–26.2, 28.1
route	M 28.1
track	M 3–4, 6
Red	J ay, P 11.2, Q 3
Reed beds	C 33
Reef	J 22, K 16, g–h, m

Reference to	
adjoining chart	A 19
charted units	A b
larger-scale chart	A 18
Reflector, radar	Q 10–11, S 4
Refuge	
beacon	Q 124
for shipwrecked mariners	T 14
Regions, IALA	Q 130.1
Relief	C 10–14
Reported	
anchorage	N 10
danger	I 4
depth	I 3.1–4
Reporting, radio	M 40.1–40.2
Rescue station	T 11–12
Reservation line	N f
Reserve fog signal	R 22
Reserved anchorage area	N 12.9
Resilient beacon	P 5
Restricted	
area	M 14, N 2.1, 20–27
light sector	P 44.1–44.2
Retroreflecting material	Q 6
Rice paddy	C n
Riprap	P a
River	C 20
intermittent	C 21
Road	D 10–11
Rock	J 9.1, K 10–15, a–b
Rocket station	T 12
Rocky	J 9.1
area which covers and uncovers	J 21
Roll-on, Roll-off ferry terminal (RoRo)	F 50
Rotating-pattern radiobeacon	S 12
Rotten	J aj
Roundabout	M 21
Route	M 27.1–28.2
Routing Measures	M 18–29.2
Rubble	C e
Ruin	D 8, F 33.1

Index

Ruined	
landmark	D 8
pier	F 33.2
S	
Safe	
clearance depth	K 3, 30, f
vertical clearance	D 26, i
water mark	Q 130.5
Safety	
fairway	M 18
zone	L 3
Sailing club	F 11.3
Salt pans	C 24
Sand	C c, J 1
Sandhills	C 8
Sandwaves	J 14
Sandy shore	C 6
Satellite Navigation System	S 50–51
Scale	A 13–15
Scanner, radar	E 30.3
Schist	J h
School	E f
Scoriae	J o
Scrubbing grid	F 24
Sea mile (nautical mile)	A 15, B 45
Seabed, types of	J 1–15, a–bf
Seagrass	J 13.3
Seal	
chart producer	A 12
sanctuary	N 22
Seaplane	
anchorage	N 14
landing area, operating area	N 13
Seasonal	
buoy	Q 71
sea ice limit	N 60.2
Sea-tangle	J w
Seawall	F 2.1–2.2
Seaward limit of	
contiguous zone	N 44
territorial sea	N 43
Second	
of arc	B 6
of time	B 51

Sector lights	P 40.1–46.2
See adjoining chart	A 19
Semaphore	T f
Semi-diurnal tide	H 30
Separation	
line	M 12
scheme	M 10–13, 20.1–29.2
zone	M 13
Services	T
Settlements	D 1–8
Sewer	L 41.1–41.2
Shading	C g
Shapes of buoys	Q 20–26
Shark nets	F 29.1
Shed, transit	F 51
Shellfish bed	K 47
Shells	J 11
Shingle	C c, J d
Shingly shore	C 7
Shoal sounding on rock	K b
Shore, shoreline	C 1–8
Short-long flashing	P b
Shrine	E 13
Signal	
fog	R
stations	T 20–36
Silo	E 33
Silt	J 4
Single	
Anchor Leg Mooring (SALM)	L 12
Buoy Mooring (SBM)	L 16
Point Mooring (SPM)	L 12
Sinker	K n
Siren	R 12
Sketches	E 3.1–3.2
Slack water	H 31
Slipway	F 23
Small	J ah
Small craft	
leisure facilities	U
mooring	Q 44
Snag	K 43.2

Soft	J 35
Sounding	I 10–16
datum	C a, b, K h
doubtful depth	I 2
out of position	I 11
unreliable	I 14
Source diagram	A 17
South	B 11
cardinal mark	Q 130.3
Southeast	B 14
Southwest	B 16
Spar buoy	Q 24
Special	
lights	P 60–66
marks	Q 130.6
purpose beacon	Q 120–126
purpose buoy	Q 50–71
Speckled	J al
Speed limit	N 27
Spherical buoy	Q 22
Spicules	J x
Spindle buoy	Q 24
Spire	E 10.3
Spoil ground	N 62.1–62.2
Sponge	J t
Spot height	C 10–11, 13, H 20
Spring	
tide	H 16, 30–31
seabed	J 15
Square	
meter	B a
shaped beacon	Q l
Stake	K 43.2, Q 90
Station	
Coast Guard	T 10–11
coast radar	M 30, S 1
DGPS, providing corrections	S 51
QTG, providing radio service	S 15
radar surveillance	M 30
radio direction finding	S 14
railway	D 13
rescue	T 11–12
signal	T 20–36
tide	H 30
Statute	E 24
Statute mile	B e

Index

Steep coast	C 3
Steps	F 18
Sticky	J 34
Stiff	J 36
Stock number	A d
Stones	C 7, J 5
area with	J 20
Stony shore	C 7
Storage tanker	L 17
Storm signal station	T 28
Straight territorial sea baseline	N 42
Strand	C c
Streaky	J ak
Stream	C 20, H l, I c
Gulf	H u
tidal signal station	T 34
tidal table	H 31, 46
tide	H 40–41
Street	D 7
Strip light	P 64
Stumps of piles/posts	K 43.1–43.2
Submarine	
cable	L 30.1–32
cable area	L 30.2
exercise area	N 33
pipeline	L 40–44
power cable	L 31.1
power cable area	L 31.2
transit lane	N 33
volcano	K d
Submerged	
crib	K i
duck blind	K k
jetty	F b
platform	K l
production well	L 20
rock, beacon on	Q 83
well (buoyed)	L a
wreck	K 22–23, 26–30
Subsidiary light	P 42.1–42.2
Subsurface Ocean Data Acquisition System (ODAS)	L 25
Sunken	
danger (swept)	K f
wreck	K c
Superbuoy	Q 26
Supply pipeline	L 40.1–40.2

Surveyed	
coastline	C 1
inadequately	I 25
Suspended well	L 21.1–21.2
Swamp	C 33
Swept	
area	I 24, b
channel	I a
wire drag, by	K 2, 27, 42, f
Swing bridge	D 23.2
Swinging circle	N 11.2
Symbolized positions	B 30–33
Synchronized light	P 66
T	
Tanker	
anchorage area	N 12.5
CALM	L 16
storage, moored	L 17
Tank	E 32
Telegraphic mooring buoy	Q 43
Telephone	E q
line	D 27
Telephonic mooring buoy	Q 43
Television	
mast	E 28
station	E 27
tower	E 29
Temple	E 13
Temporary	
buoy (seasonal)	Q 71
light	P 54
Tenacious	J aq
Terms relating to tidal levels	H 1–17, a–k
Territorial Sea	N 42–43
Tidal	
basin	F 28
harbor	F 28
levels	H 1–17, 20
stream	H 1
signal station	T 34
station	H 46
table	A g, H 31
streams and currents	H 40–47
table	H 30
Tide	
gauge	T 32.1–32.2
level terms	H 1–17, a–k
rips	H 44

scale	T 32.1
signal station	T 33
table	A g, H 30–31
Timber yard	F 52
Time	
signal station	T 31
units of	B 49–51
Tomb	E b
Ton, tonnage, tonne (weight)	B 53, m
Topmark	Q 9–11, 82, 102.1
Tower	E 20
beacon	P 3, Q 110–111
church	E 10.2
radar	E 30.2
radio	E 29
television	E 29
water	E 21
Track	D 12, M 1–6, 27.3
Traffic	
separation scheme (TSS)	M 10–15, 20–26.2
basic symbols	M 10–15
example	M 18–29.2
signal station	T 21–22, 25.1
surveillance station	M 30
Training wall	F 5
Transhipment	
area	N 64
facilities	F 50–53.2
Transit	
lane (submarine)	N 33
line	M 2
shed	F 51
Transmission line	D 26–27, h
Transmitter, AIS	S 17.1–17.2
Transponder beacon	S 3.1–3.6
Transporter	
bridge	D 24
overhead (aerial cableway)	D 25
Trap, fish	K 44.2–45, Q i
Traveling crane	F 53.1
Trees	
height of top	C 14
types of	C 31–32, i–k
Triangular shaped beacon	Q l
Triangulation point	B 20
Trot, mooring	Q 42
True (compass)	B s

Index

Tufa	J n
Tun buoy	Q 25
Tunnel	D 16
pipeline	L 42.2
Tunney nets	K 44.2–45
area	K 45
Turbine	
wind	E 26.1, L 5.1
underwater	L 24
Two-way	
route	M 27.2, 28.1–28.2
track	M 4, 5.2
Tyfon	R 13
Types of	
fog signals	R 10–16
seabed, intertidal areas	J 20–22

U

Ultra quick light	P 10.8
Uncovers	K 11, 21, h
Under construction	D d, F 30–32
Underwater	
installations	L 20–25
rock	K 13–15
turbine	L 24
Uneven	J bf
Unexploded ordinance	K p
Units	A b, B 40–54
University	E h
Unsurveyed	
coastline	C 2
depths	I 25
Unwatched, unmanned light	P 53, e
Update	A 7
Upper light	P 22
Urban area	D 1

V

Variation, magnetic	B 68.1–71, p
Varied	J be
Various limits	N 60.1–65
Vegetation	C 30–33, i–t
Velocity	H n

Vertical	
clearance	D 22, 23.1, 23.4, 23.6–28
color striped	Q 5
lights	P 15
Vertically disposed	P 15
Very quick light	P 10.7
Vessel, light	P e
Viaduct	D f
Views	E 3.1–3.2
Village	D 4
Violet	J at, P 11.5
Virtual AIS	S 18.1–18.7
Visitor's	
berth	F 19.2
mooring	Q 45
Volcanic	J 37
ash	J k
Volcano	K d

W

Wall, training	F 5
Warehouse	F 51
Water	
discolored	K e
features	C 20–25
intake	L 41.1–41.2, b
pipeline	L 40.1, 41.1
pipeline area	L 40.2, L 41.2
tank	E 21
tower	E 21
Waterfalls	C 22
Watermill	E c
Wave	
actuated fog signal	R 21–22
farm	L 6
Way point	M 40.1
Weather signal station	T 29
Weed	J 13.1–13.2
Weir, fish	K 44.2
Well	E e
submerged	L a
suspended	L 21
production	L 20
Wellhead	L 21.1–21.2, 23
West	B 12
cardinal mark	Q 130.3

Wet dock	F 27
Wharf	F 13
Whistle	R 15
buoy	Q c
White	J ar, P 11.1
Wind	
farm	E 26.2, L 5.2
signal station	T 29
turbine	E 26.1, L 5.1
Windmill	E 25.1–25.2
Withy	Q 91–92
Woodland	
coniferous	C j
deciduous	C i
Woods, wooded	C 30
Works	
at sea, (reclamation area)	F 31
on land	F 30
under construction, works in progress	F 32
World Geodetic System (WGS)	S 50
Wreck	K 20–30, c
buoy (marking new danger)	Q 130.7
mast	K 25

Y

Yacht	
berths without facilities	F 11.2
club	F 11.3
Yard	B d
timber	F 52
Yellow	J aw, P 11.6

Z

Zone	
Exclusive Economic Zone (EEZ)	N 47
fishing	N 45
inshore traffic	M 25.1–25.2
seaward, contiguous	N 44
separation	M 13, 20.1–20.3

Appendix 1   IALA Maritime Buoyage System

Region A   (North America = Region B (see Map p. 99)
Lateral Marks

| Port Hand | | Starboard Hand | Preferred Channel to Starboard | | Preferred Channel to Port |

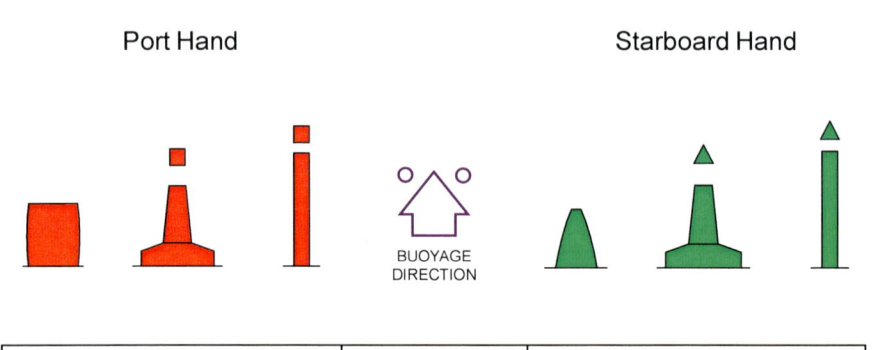

red	Color	green
cylindrical (can), pillar, spar	Buoy	conical (nun), pillar, spar
single red cylinder (can)	Topmark (if any)	single green cone, point upward

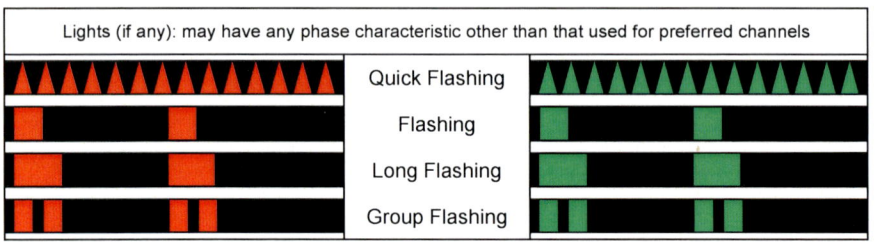

red with one green horizontal band	Color	green with one red horizontal band
cylindrical (can), pillar, spar	Buoy	conical (nun), pillar, spar
single red cylinder (can)	Topmark (if any)	single green cone, point upward

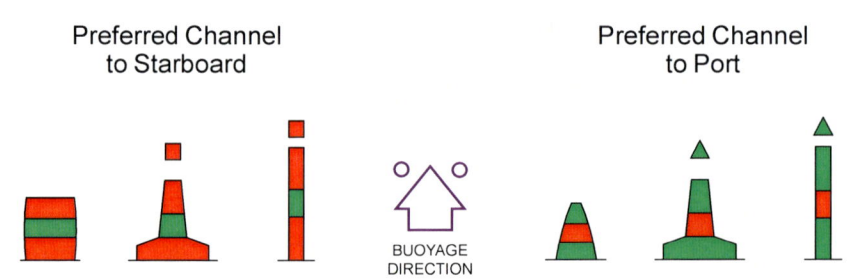

128

IALA Maritime Buoyage System — Appendix 1

Region B (North America = Region B (see Map p. 99)
Lateral Marks

Port Hand / Starboard Hand

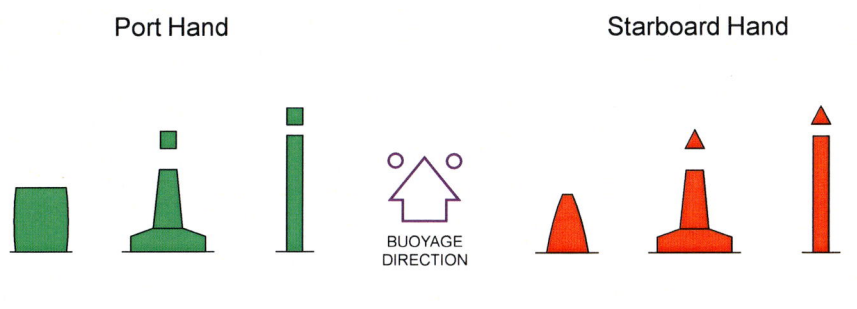

	Color	
green		red
cylindrical (can), pillar, spar	Buoy	conical (nun), pillar, spar
single green cylinder (can)	Topmark (if any)	single red cone, point upward

Lights (if any): may have any phase characteristic other than that used for preferred channels

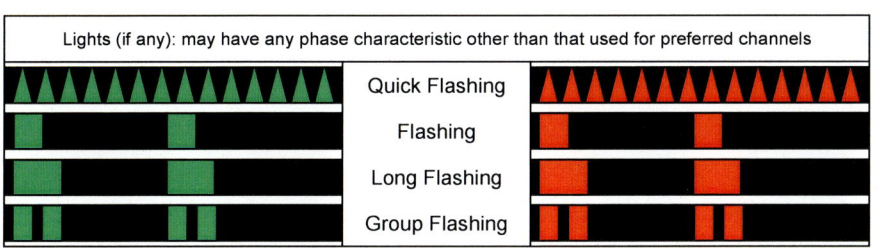

Preferred Channel to Starboard / Preferred Channel to Port

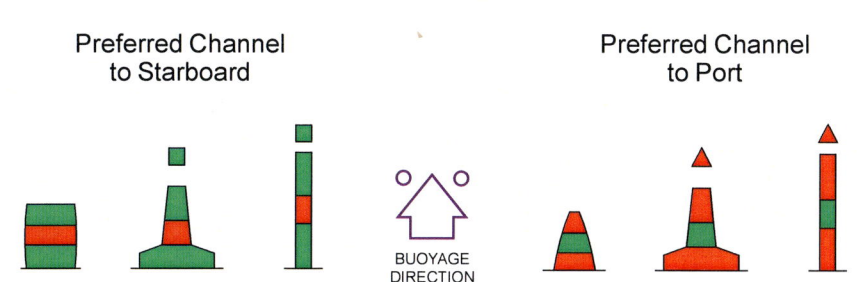

	Color	
green with one red horizontal band		red with one green horizontal band
cylindrical (can), pillar, spar	Buoy	conical (nun), pillar, spar
single green cylinder (can)	Topmark (if any)	single red cone, point upward

Lights (if any) are composite group flashing

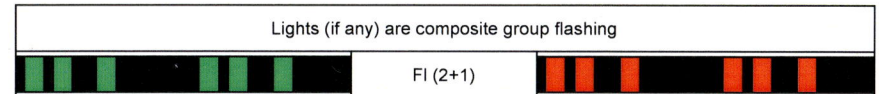

Fl (2+1)

Appendix 1   IALA Maritime Buoyage System

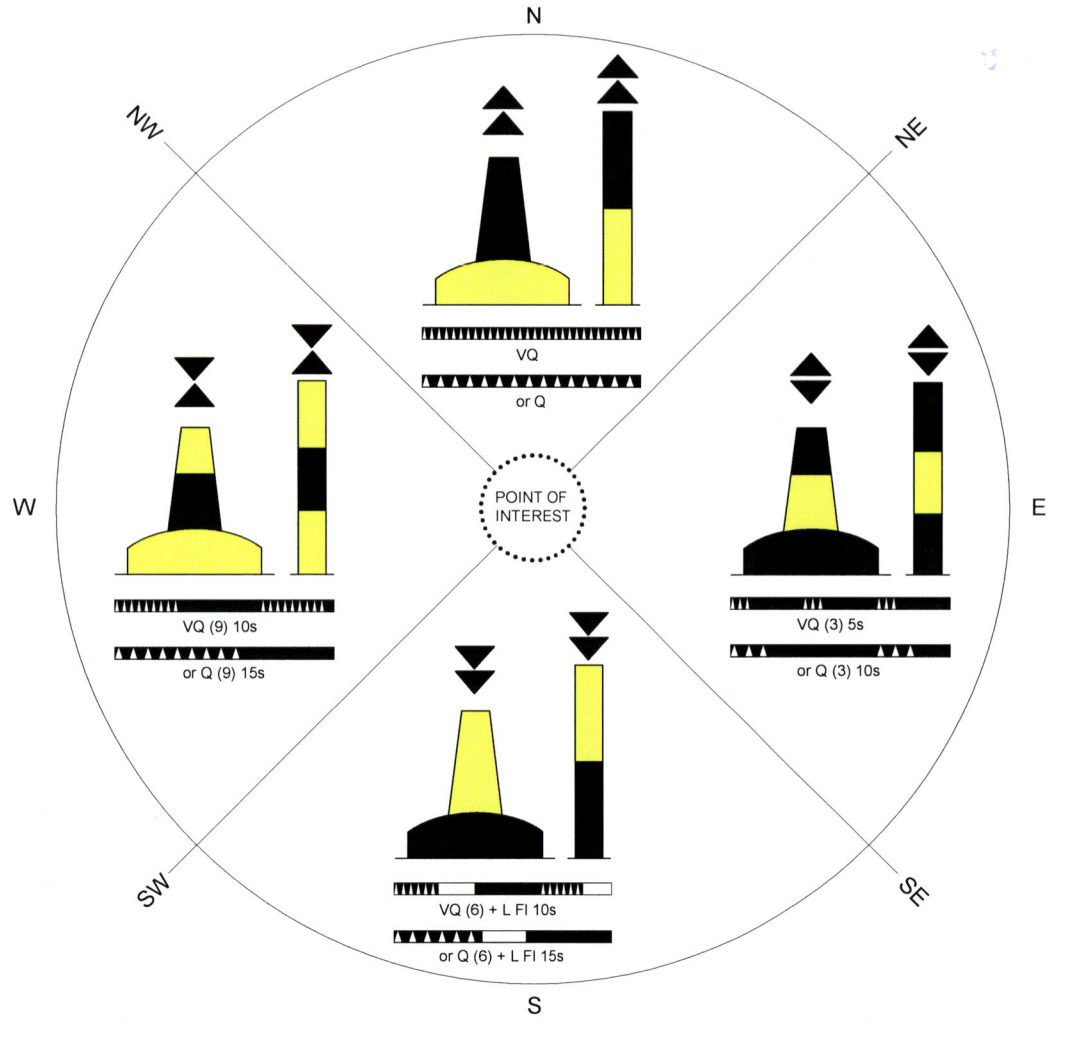

IALA Maritime Buoyage System — Appendix 1

Regions A and B

Isolated Danger Marks

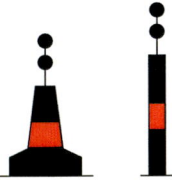

Color	black with one or more red horizontal band(s)
Buoy	optional, but not conflicting with lateral marks; pillar or spar preferred
Topmark (if any)	always fitted with double spheres

Lights (if any)	
Color	white
Rhythm	group flashing

Safe Water Marks

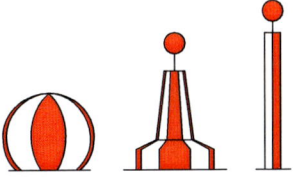

Color	red and white vertical stripes
Buoy	spherical, pillar or spar
Topmark (if any)	single red sphere

white	
ISO	
Oc	
L Fl 10s	
Morse "A"	

Special Marks

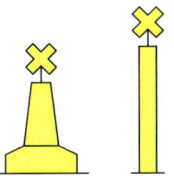

Color	yellow
Buoy	optional, but not conflicting with lateral marks
Topmark (if any)	single yellow "X" shape

yellow	
Fl Y	
Fl (4) Y	

May have any rhythm other than those used for white lights on cardinal, isolated danger or safe water marks.

New Danger Marks

Color	blue and yellow vertical stripes
Buoy	pillar or spar
Topmark (if any)	vertical/perpendicular yellow cross

alternating blue and yellow	
Al Oc Bu Y 3s	

Record of Corrections

Notice No.	Corrected on	Corrected by	Notice No.	Corrected on	Corrected by	Notice No.	Corrected on	Corrected by